To Clifford Bamfield

Foreword

The survival of London's City churches is a miracle. Though a few medieval structures remain the overwhelming majority rose from the ruins of the Great Fire to form a complete set of late-17th century places of worship. They defied the Blitz and the equally severe threat of post-war commercial development. However tiny, however inconvenient and however forlorn, they stood out against destruction. They were the one City institution capable of outgunning profit. Their sites were sacrosanct. Today they are precious beyond price. The City churches humanise the most carelessly inhumane area of the metropolis. They offer a place of repose and glory, a link to the past and a reassurance for the future that all is not lost to change.

Simon Jenkins

All Hallows by the Tower, font cover

Preface

This book is intended as an informative, easy to understand, introduction to the churches of the City of London, for the benefit of the many tourists, guides and other visitors who seek information to help them to enjoy and appreciate these wonderful buildings.

In deciding how much information to include, I have restricted myself to commenting on those things that will help the visitor to focus on the most notable and interesting features of each church. I have categorised them, for the sake of simplicity, under the headings of History, Exterior, and Interior, to which I have added a Summary which gives additional, often informal and anecdotal information, which I hope will give a more general understanding and help to put each church in some kind of context.

For the sake of brevity, when using bullet-points, I have also used some simple and, I hope, obvious abbreviations, notably WW2 for the Second World War, dem. for demolished and, for example, C17 for the seventeenth century.

I am indebted to Paul Taylor and the late Clifford Bamfield, for their valuable comments and suggestions – both taught me a great deal about the City churches. I also owe a debt to the Friends of the City Churches (FCC), who have made the publication of this book possible and without whom some of the churches might not exist today. The public would certainly find it much harder to gain access to many of the churches without the dedication of the FCC churchwatchers, who give up their time to ensure that as many as possible are kept open on a regular basis. Most of the churches are open on weekdays and full information can be found on the FCC website (www.london-city-churches.org.uk) or from The Friends of the City Churches, The Church of St Magnus the Martyr, Lower Thames Street, London EC3R 6DN.

Finally, a plea to you, the visitor. Many of the City churches have no parish and no regular source of income. In almost all cases, no charge is made for visiting them. Any donation that you make will assist these churches in paying for the considerable cost of their upkeep and will help to ensure that they continue to survive for the benefit of future visitors and worshippers.

Tony Tucker
March 2009

Introduction
A Brief History of the City Churches

London in Roman and Saxon times

London, or Londinium as it was called by the Romans, was founded soon after the invasion of Britain by the Romans, under the Emperor Claudius, in AD43. They established their settlement between the two hills of Ludgate and Cornhill, beside which were the navigable rivers Walbrook and Fleet. This was also the lowest point at which the river Thames could be forded and what was to become the Pool of London offered a reasonably deep water port for the Roman ships.

There are legends of Christian worship in the City from the 1st century onwards, but no surviving evidence. During the Saxon period, in the 9th and 10th centuries, a number of the present City churches came into existence, but the only standing Saxon fabric that survives in situ is in the west end of All Hallows by the Tower and was exposed by Second World War bombing.

The Medieval churches

From Norman times, physical evidence of churches in the City is available to us. The 11th century crypt in St Mary le Bow and the great 12th century monastic church of St Bartholomew the Great provide fine examples of Norman architecture, with its strength and simplicity, its round columns and arches.

The birth of the Gothic style, with its elegant pointed arches, can be seen in the round 12th century nave of the Temple Church, where Norman and Gothic are combined. For the next 400 years, up until Tudor times, the Gothic style held sway. Relatively few churches have survived from those years and they are mainly to be found in the east and north-east of the City, the areas largely untouched by the Great Fire of 1666. St Helen Bishopsgate and St Olave Hart Street are good examples.

Between the Reformation and the Great Fire, very little new church-building took place. In the City, one of the few was St Katharine Cree, 1628-31, which exhibits characteristics of both the Gothic style and the Classical style which was starting to become the fashion, its leading proponent in England being the great architect, Inigo Jones.

The Wren churches

One of the most important watersheds in the City's history began early in the morning of 2nd September, 1666, when the Great Fire started in the baker's shop of Thomas Farynor in Pudding Lane. By the time the conflagration had run its course, five days later, over four-fifths of the medieval City had been destroyed and, of 107 churches, some 86 had been burnt down or damaged beyond repair.

Of the 51 churches that were rebuilt, almost all were designed by the office of Christopher Wren, who had already gained the favour of King Charles II. Born in 1632, the son of a country parson, Wren was not trained as an architect, but he was a mathematician and astronomer of genius. Over the remaining years of the century, in addition to the City churches and St Paul's Cathedral, Wren was responsible for the Royal Hospitals at Chelsea and Greenwich, palaces at Whitehall, Kensington, Winchester and Hampton Court and several buildings in Oxford and Cambridge Universities, including the magnificent Tom Tower in Christ Church, Oxford and the classically elegant Trinity College Library in Cambridge.

As there had been so little church-building since the Reformation, Wren lacked any recent precedent for his church designs. He favoured the Classical style, although there were instances where he built in Gothic, either to make use of material that had survived the Fire, or to comply with the wishes of parishioners or benefactors. He believed that people going to church should be able to see and hear the service, so he gave prominence to the pulpit, installed plain glass windows and ensured that the altar was clearly visible to the congregation.

With regard to the exterior design of his churches, Wren was limited in what he could do. The City was rebuilt on the old street patterns, so he found himself working with oddly shaped and restricted plots of land on which many of the churches had stood, mostly hemmed in by houses and offices and therefore not always visible from the neighbouring streets. With money in short supply, (most of the cost of rebuilding the churches was paid for by a tax on coal), he built simple, cheap exterior walls, except where they faced on to a prominent thoroughfare, when he would design an elegant façade, such as the east wall of St Lawrence Jewry.

In most cases, Wren delayed adding steeples to his towers until he had addressed the urgent need of rebuilding the main body of a church and tower to provide a place for worship. When he did turn his attention to the steeples, and this could be 20 or 30 years later, he showed the full extent of his genius. The steeples were usually the only parts of the churches that could be seen above the surrounding buildings in the narrow streets and Wren designed an almost infinite variety that would adorn the London sky-line and provide a series of counterpoints to the massive dome of St Paul's.

Wren's interiors also show amazing variety. No two are quite the same and the designs range from great barrel-vaulted basilicas, like St Bride Fleet Street, to simple, flat-roofed interiors, without aisles, such as St Edmund King and Martyr. There are churches with one aisle and with two aisles, churches with domes and churches with galleries. Some are longitudinally planned, in traditional English style, some centrally planned, using a Greek cross design. All of them had fine furnishings and fittings, provided by the many outstanding master-craftsmen employed by Wren to decorate his church interiors.

Although Wren had overall responsibility for the design and building of the City churches, he clearly did not undertake every individual design himself, nor could he have done, given the many other buildings for which he was responsible. He was supported by other architects and surveyors, most notably the multi-talented Robert Hooke and, later on, the innovative Nicholas Hawksmoor. Their influence can be detected in many of the church designs, but it was Wren who was ultimately accountable for the results.

Of the 50 churches attributed to Wren, only 23 survive and some of these were heavily restored in the 19th century or after the Second World War. There are a further two ruined churches and four towers by Wren.

The Post-Wren churches

In the 18th and 19th centuries, several fine churches were built, to the design of various architects. Hawksmoor's St Mary Woolnoth is a powerful and original church and the works of George Dance Senior (St Botolph Aldgate) and his son, George Dance Junior (All Hallows London Wall) are very attractive buildings. Other architects, such as Nathaniel Wright (St Botolph Aldersgate) and John Shaw Senior (St Dunstan in the West) also left their mark in impressive style.

As the 19th century progressed, however, a significant change took place in the City. The arrival of the railways led to the migration of large numbers of City dwellers to the rapidly growing suburbs and the age of the commuter was born. Congregations of the City churches fell dramatically and there was accordingly no need for the same number of churches as in the past, when there had been a church on almost every street, some serving very small parishes.

From the 1860s onwards, churches began to be demolished and the money raised from the sale of the sites used to fund the building of new churches in the suburbs. Many well-known churches disappeared in this way, among them St Antholin, one of Wren's finest church buildings, which was knocked down in 1874-75. Other churches were substantially altered as the Victorian restorers went about their work, introducing changes to the interiors of a number of the City churches.

The aftermath of the Second World War

Apart from the Great Fire, no event caused more damage to the City churches than the bombing suffered by London in the 1939-45 war. Only a few churches escaped unscathed and some were destroyed completely, including Wren's beautiful St Mildred Bread Street. Others were left as shells and some of the churchyards were turned into gardens. A few towers were left to stand on their own, some of which were put to new uses, such as St Alban Wood Street (a private residence), St Olave Jewry (offices) and St Augustine (part of St Paul's Cathedral School).

Many of the bombed churches were rebuilt or have been restored since the war to adapt them for their modern uses. Some of these restorations have been sympathetic to the architect's original intentions, others less so, but at least we still have these churches with us to enjoy today.

The Templeman Report and the re-founding of the Friends of the City Churches

In the 1990s, another threat to the City churches emerged from a quite different source. The Templeman Report into the need for, and future use of, the churches, recommended the retention of only some of the existing churches, the remainder being deemed surplus to requirements.

Fearing for the future of these churches, the Friends of the City Churches was re-founded (it had existed many years earlier) with the aim of preserving, publicising and fostering the well-being of the churches that remained. Today, over 40 churches survive in the City, many of which still provide for the spiritual needs of the City's residents and workers, but others have been put to new uses, serving non-Anglican communities, for instance, or acting as centres for ecumenical groups. Although not all are regularly open to the public, the Friends of the City Churches provide "watchers" in an increasing number of them, so that most can be visited at some time during the week.

Just as they have adapted and survived in the past, the City churches promise to be with us in the future, offering a service to those who need it. They not only give an insight into the lives of past communities in the great City of London, but also provide evidence of the skills and workmanship of those who designed and built them.

KEY TO MAP

Church/palce of worship	map number	page number

Churches

Ruined Churches

Towers Only

Other Places of Worship in or close to the City

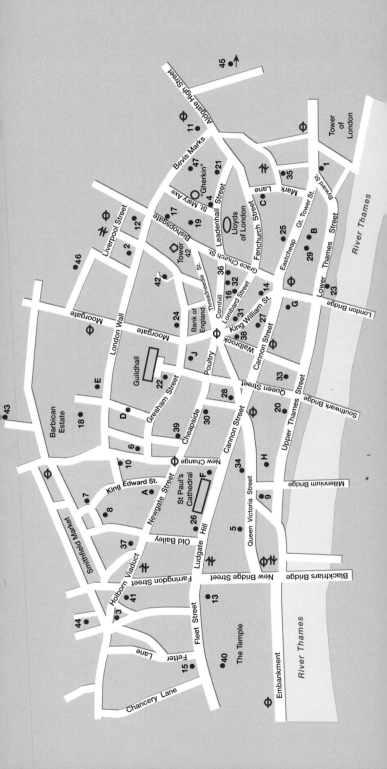

All Hallows by the Tower
Byward Street

History

- Also called All Hallows Barking, having been founded by St Ethelburga and the nuns of Barking Abbey

- Escaped damage in the Great Fire, the tower famously being used as a vantage point to view the Fire by Samuel Pepys

- Gutted by bombing in WW2 and rebuilt by Lord Mottistone in the 1950s

- Bomb damage exposed Saxon remains and a crypt containing a Roman pavement

Exterior

- Stands on an island site close to the Tower of London

- Red brick tower dating from mid-C17 with modern steeple covered in Zambian copper

- North and south walls dating from C15

Interior

- C15 aisle walls, with concrete ceiling and limestone piers by Lord Mottistone

- Saxon arch in south-west (the only standing Saxon fabric to be seen in a London church)

- Baptistery in south-west corner, with exquisite font cover of over 100 pieces by Grinling Gibbons, carved with cherubs supporting flowers, leaves, wheat-ears and fir-cones, topped by a dove

- Modern stained glass baptistery windows by Keith New

- Altar-piece in north aisle with four painted Flemish panels from nearby late C15 chantry founded by Alderman Sir Robert Tate

- Wren-period pulpit from St Swithin London Stone (dem. 1940), with large modern tester

- Many fine monuments and 17 brasses

- Extensive undercroft, with a museum of the church's history, including many Roman and Saxon remains

- Mariners Chapel in south-east, with cross made of wood from the Cutty Sark and an ivory figure of Christ from the flagship of the Spanish Amada

- Three outstanding sword-rests

Summary

All Hallows by the Tower is a church steeped in historical associations. Although Second World War bombing caused extensive damage, it also revealed the Roman and Saxon remains which are of so much interest to today's visitor. The sensitive rebuilding of the church has created a light and spacious interior in which the surviving fabric and furnishings can be admired.

The church has connections with many famous people and events: William Penn was baptised here; his father and Samuel Pepys destroyed local houses to protect the church from the Great Fire; John Quincy Adams (6th President of the USA) was married in the church, as was the infamous Judge Jeffreys; and the former Rector, Tubby Clayton, founded the Toc H movement (the Toc H lamp can be seen on the tomb of Alderman John Croke in the Toc H Chapel in the north aisle)

All Hallows is also home to one of the more fascinating of the many historic City ceremonies which take place each year. The Knollys Rose ceremony, in which the Lord Mayor is presented with a single rose, commemorates an event in 1381 when Sir Robert Knollys was ordered to pay a fine of one red rose for the offence, allegedly committed by his wife, of building an unauthorised bridge over Seething Lane between two of his properties.

All Hallows London Wall

London Wall

History

- First mentioned c.1130, built next to north perimeter of the City wall

- Survived the Great Fire and rebuilt by George Dance the Younger, 1765-67

- Some restoration in late C19 and again, after severe bomb damage in WW2, by David Nye in 1960-62

Exterior

- Plain brown brick walls with semi-circular windows at clerestory level and a rounded apse at the east end

- Projecting tower of Portland stone with delicate cupola and Tuscan doorway, facing a small churchyard garden

Interior

- Simple nave without aisles. Barrel-vaulted ceiling springing from engaged Ionic columns and decorated with plaster motifs

- Diagonally coffered apse, inspired by the Temple of Venus and Rome in the Forum in Rome

- Large oil painting above the altar by Dance's brother, Sir Nathaniel Dance-Holland, a copy of an early C17 Italian painting by Pietro da Cortona

- West gallery on Tuscan columns, with attractive modern organ by Noel Mander in late C19 case from Islington Town Hall, originally made for a private house in Highbury

- Royal Arms, c.1700, on front of west gallery

- Unusual pulpit on north wall, only accessible from outside the church, through the vestry

- Late C17 font from St Mary Magdalen Old Fish Street (dem. 1886), by way of St Paul's Cathedral

- Chandelier given by a parishioner in 1766

- Wrought iron sword-rest, 1753

Summary

The contrast between the plain exterior of this church and the exquisite interior could hardly be greater. The tower and cupola are very attractive, but the south wall, facing the street, is rather severe.

It is a surprise, therefore, to find inside the church such a beautiful and original design, particularly when one considers that it was George Dance the Younger's first building and that he was only 24 years old at the time. The coffered ceiling with delicate patterns reminiscent of snowflakes is well-lit by clerestory windows and the decorated ceiling of the apse is quite captivating.

Like the rest of the interior, the furnishings are simple and elegant, the chandelier in the apse and the organ gallery at the west end being particularly noteworthy. A most unusual feature is the pulpit, the only one in a City church which has to be entered from outside the nave, through a vestry which is built on part of the original Roman City wall.

St Andrew Holborn

Holborn Circus

History

- First mentioned c.959 in King Edgar's renewal of the Charter of Westminster Abbey

- Survived the Great Fire, but became dilapidated and rebuilt by Wren, 1684-86

- Major restoration by S. S. Teulon, 1869-72, radically altering the interior

- Gutted by bombing in WW2 and restored by Lord Mottistone of Seeley and Paget

Exterior

- A large church faced with Portland stone and situated on an island site, entered through an attractive garden created in 1970

- C15 tower re-faced by Wren in 1703 with elaborate round-headed belfry windows

- C17 stone carving of The Last Judgement on north wall, formerly above entrance to burial ground

- Statues of charity children on west wall, similar to those in St Bride and in St Botolph Bishopsgate parish hall

Interior

- Vestibule beneath tower with C15 arches

- Barrel-vaulted nave and wide, groin-vaulted north and south aisles with galleries

- West organ gallery with organ case from the chapel of the Foundling Hospital, given by Handel in 1750

- C19 pulpit and font also from the Foundling Hospital chapel

- Post-war reredos, modelled on Wren's original

- Stained glass east window, The Last Supper and Ascension by Brian Thomas, 1961

- More stained glass by Thomas in north-west chapel, which also contains altar-rails and part of reredos, c.1733, from St Luke Old Street

- Tomb of Captain Thomas Coram, founder of the C18 Foundling Hospital, at west end

Summary

This is Wren's largest parish church and was well restored, on the lines of the original, after the destruction of the interior by bombing in 1941.

The church stands in an attractive garden which is entered through fine wrought iron gates. Above the tower doorway are the statues of two charity children from the parochial school in Hatton Garden. The church also has connections with the Foundling Hospital established in the 18th century by Captain Thomas Coram, whose tomb is to be seen inside the church.

The interior is one of Wren's great basilica designs, with a lofty coloured and gilded plasterwork ceiling and galleries supported on wooden columns, with Corinthian columns above.

Benjamin Disraeli was baptised here in 1817. It is said that his father, angry at having a fine imposed on him for refusing the position of Warden at Bevis Marks synagogue, brought his son to be christened at St Andrew Holborn as a protest.

St Andrew Undershaft

St Mary Axe, off Leadenhall Street

History

- Named after the maypole which once stood higher than the church tower on May Days and which was taken down permanently after riots in 1517 and later destroyed as a pagan idol

- First mentioned in the early C12, the present building mostly of c.1520 origin

- Survived both the Great Fire and WW2, but suffered damage from IRA bomb in 1992

Exterior

- C15 south-west tower, with pinnacles and stair-turret added in late C19

- The rest of the exterior mostly typical C16 Perpendicular style

Interior

- Six-bay nave with aisles and clerestory

- High ceiling with flat panels, rebuilt in 1950, showing date of 1532 on one of the corbels

- Fine late C17 pulpit

- Renatus Harris organ from 1690s

- Wrought iron communion rails by Jean Tijou, 1704

- Two sword-rests displayed on the wall of a room in the tower, one originally from All Hallows Staining (dem. 1870)

- West window with shields of five C15/C16 monarchs replacing C17 window largely destroyed by 1992 bomb

- East window by Heaton, Butler and Bayne, 1875-6, showing Crucifixion and Ascension

- Aisle windows with heraldic glass dating from 1530

- Several fine monuments, including: (north-east corner) John Stow, 1605, author of the Survey of London, shown sitting at a writing desk and holding quill pen; (north wall) Sir Hugh Hammersley, 1636, large wall-monument showing the former Lord Mayor in armour, with kneeling figures under curtains, Alice Byng, 1616, kneeling figure high on wall; (chancel) Sir Thomas Offley, 1582, kneeling figures at a prayer desk

Summary

St Andrew Undershaft is one of the City's medieval churches situated in an area that escaped most of the devastation caused by the Great Fire and the War, although it suffered some damage from the IRA bomb in 1992, notably to its fine 17th century west window.

Having been overshadowed on May Days until Tudor times by a giant maypole, it is today dwarfed by the "Gherkin", which rises close behind it, whilst across the street stands the famous Lloyd's building.

The church has a light and spacious Perpendicular style interior and is known for its connection with John Stow, whose fine monument is the focus of one of the City's historic ceremonies, in which Stow's quill pen is replaced every three years. There is also a commemorative plaque on the south wall to the painter, Hans Holbein, who lived nearby.

In recent years, the church has been used on a daily basis by a young Christian group in the City.

St Andrew by the Wardrobe

Queen Victoria Street

History

- Named after the nearby King's Wardrobe, where the monarch's clothing and other stores were housed from the mid-C14 until the Great Fire in 1666

- Rebuilt by Wren, 1685-94

- Gutted by incendiary bombs in WW2 and restored by Marshall Sisson, 1959-61

Exterior

- Prominent position above Queen Victoria Street

- Original C17 red brick tower and walls, with quoins

- Weathervane from St Michael Bassishaw (dem. 1900)

Interior

- Barrel-vaulted in original Wren style

- Galleries on three sides, with aisles enclosed at floor level by wood panelling

- Pulpit, font and font cover from St Matthew Friday Street (dem. 1884)

- Early C18 chandeliers made of latten (a compound of zinc, lead and tin)

- Two small wooden sculptures in sanctuary, St Andrew, c.1600 and St Ann holding Virgin and Child, c.1500

- Stained glass panel in west gallery showing Conversion of St Paul, by Joshua Price, early C18; modern south aisle windows by Carl Edwards

- Etched glass panel in vestibule depicting St Andrew's and other churches saved by the politician Ivor Bulmer Thomas

- Royal Arms of c.1685 above tower doorway, from St Olave Jewry (dem. 1888)

- Interesting picture of Blackfriars monastery and surrounding area on south staircase to west gallery

- Memorial reliefs in west gallery to Shakespeare, who lived in Ireland Yard, close to the church, and his contemporary, John Dowland, composer and lutenist to James I. Also a picture of Van Dyck, who had a studio nearby

Summary

St Andrew by the Wardrobe is today far more prominent than it would have been before the building of Queen Victoria Street in the early 1870s. The best view is from the balcony in front of Richard Kindersley's "Seven Ages of Man" sculpture on the raised plaza of Baynard House, on the other side of the street. Although the church was badly damaged in the War, the elegant red brick tower and walls are all Wren's original work.

The restoration of the basilica style interior by Marshall Sisson is in sympathy with the Wren original. A number of 17th and 18th century furnishings have been introduced from other churches. Above the nave hang six flags of institutions with which the church has connections: the Diocese of London; the City of London; the companies of the Mercers, the Blacksmiths and the Parish Clerks; and the Apothecaries Society.

The west gallery contains several items of interest, including reminders of local connections with Shakespeare and Van Dyck, as well as a picture of the area in mediaeval times, showing, among other important buildings, the Blackfriars monastery, Baynard's and Montfichet castles and Bridewell Palace.

St Anne and St Agnes
Gresham Street

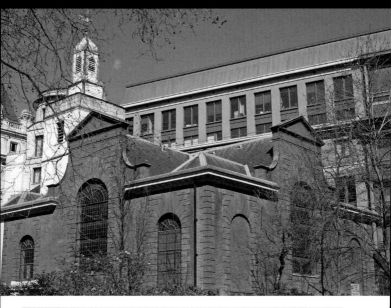

History

- Dedicated to St Anne, mother of the Virgin Mary, and St Agnes, who, at age 13, was one of the youngest Christian martyrs

- Rebuilt by Wren, 1677-87

- Badly damaged by bombing in WW2. Sensitively restored, 1963-68, by Braddock and Martin Smith and leased since that time to the Lutheran Church

Exterior

- Set behind a delightful garden, close to the north-west edge of the Roman City wall

- Small, stuccoed tower, rebuilt by Wren on the lower stages of the C14 tower, which survived the Great Fire. Topped by a weatherboarded bell turret with weathervane in shape of the letter "A"

- Warm red brick walls on south and east, stuccoed on the north, all with large, plain glass, round-headed windows flanked by smaller ones, each surrounded with rusticated brickwork

Interior

- Centralised design, with Greek cross-in-a-square, the four barrel-vaulted arms meeting in a groin-vaulted central section, supported on four Corinthian columns

- Original reredos by a local parishioner, with paintings on either side of Moses and Aaron from St Michael, Wood Street (dem. 1894)

- Pulpit incorporating panels by Jonathan Maine from St Augustine, Watling Street (destroyed, except for tower, in WW2)

- South doorcase from Dunster Castle, Somerset, with a broken pediment supported on engaged Corinthian columns and topped by a finely carved gilt angel from St Mildred Bread Street (destroyed in WW2)

- West doorcase with the tiny figure of Father Time, complete with sickle and hour-glass, also from St Mildred Bread Street

- Exceptionally fine Royal Arms of Charles II from St Mary Whitechapel (destroyed in WW2) above west door

Summary

The only City church with a double dedication, St Anne and St Agnes is a beautifully restored Wren building, probably modelled on the Nieuwe Kerk in Haarlem and with an interior similar in style to those at St Martin Ludgate and St Mary at Hill.

The exterior, with its distinctive red brick, seen through a garden on the corner of Gresham Street and Noble Street, has a distinctly Dutch feel to it. The small and friendly interior, although mostly a post-war restoration, has a number of 17th century furnishings, brought from a variety of other churches which were either demolished by the Victorians or destroyed in the Blitz.

Now a Lutheran church, services are conducted in Estonian, Latvian and Swahili, as well as English. St Anne and St Agnes is also known for its lunch-time recitals and has a particular reputation for featuring the music of Bach.

St Bartholomew the Great
West Smithfield

History

- Dedicated to St Bartholomew, one of the Apostles, whose emblem is the flaying knife, the instrument of his martyrdom

- Founded in 1123 by Rahere, a courtier of King Henry I, who, whilst on a pilgrimage to Rome, was saved from malaria and, in a vision, was instructed by the saint to build a priory on the "smooth field", now known as Smithfield

- After destruction of the nave in the Reformation, c.1543, the parish took over the choir and crossing from the new owner, Sir Richard Rich, as their church

- South-west tower added in 1628

- Restoration by Sir Aston Webb, 1886-98

Exterior

- Approached through a restored Tudor gateway, incorporating the C13 west doorway to the south aisle of the priory

- C19 porch and west front in flint and Portland stone, by Webb, with C17 red-brick tower and wooden lantern above the south aisle

- East side of original C12 cloister, restored in C15, situated on south side of nave

Interior

- Massive Norman arches in the original choir of the priory church, plus the crossing and first bay of the old nave and Webb's north and south transepts

- Vaulted aisles, triforium and C14 clerestory with C14 Lady Chapel behind the apse (restored by Webb) and vaulted crypt below

- Round Norman arches on east and west sides of crossing, pointed Gothic arches on north and south, all from C12

- Prior Bolton's oriel window, c.1517, in south gallery, with rebus (pictorial pun) of an arrow ("bolt") piercing a wine barrel ("tun")

- Rare early C15 octagonal font

- Fine wrought iron screen to the Lady Chapel, made by Starkie Gardner in 1897

- C15 canopied tomb-chest to Rahere (d. 1144) on north-east side of chancel with recumbent figure in habit of the Augustinian canons

- Many other fine monuments on north and south walls

Summary

One of the oldest of the surviving City churches, St Bartholomew the Great is the outstanding Norman church in London and, despite many restorations, retains much of its original fabric.

Founded in 1123 by Rahere, who also founded the neighbouring hospital, its dark and powerful interior still has a monastic feel about it. Having partially survived the Reformation, the church fell into a state of decay during the following centuries, when different parts of the building were put to a variety of secular uses. These included a school in the triforium, stables in the cloisters, a blacksmith's shop in the north transept (hence the blackened walls) and a printing shop in the Lady Chapel, in which Benjamin Franklin worked in 1724.

In more recent times, the church has been used as a film set, featuring in Four Weddings and a Funeral and Shakespeare in Love.

History

- Originally, from 1184, a chapel attached to St Bartholomew's Hospital, founded by Rahere in 1123, at the same time as the neighbouring priory

- The parish church of the hospital since the re-founding of the latter in c.1546, after the dissolution of the monasteries

- Reconstructed as a wooden octagon in 1789-91 by George Dance the Younger

- Rebuilt in stone and iron by Thomas Hardwick, 1823-25, with further restoration by his grandson, Philip Hardwick, 1862-63

- Badly damaged in WW2 and restored by Lord Mottistone, 1950-51

Exterior

- C15 tower with south-west stair turret, situated just inside the hospital gates

- West vestry also surviving from the C15

- C19 octagonal nave

Interior

- Entrance through tower, with vestry on left, featuring original floor and C15 arches

- Octagonal nave with pointed clerestory windows and star-shaped plaster rib-vault

- Pews and fittings mostly Victorian, with alabaster pulpit by Philip Hardwick

- 1969 doorway for invalid chairs (south end of east wall)

- Walls covered with memorials to doctors, nurses and other staff of the hospital

- Memorial on north wall to Lady Ann Bodley, wife of founder of the Bodleian Library in Oxford

- Stained glass east window by Hugh Easton, 1950

- Paintings in vestry of the Crucifixion, by Cigoli, c.1600 and St Bartholomew, C17 Spanish or Italian

- Also in vestry, brass to William Markeby and wife, 1439; four C15 carved angels with shields; and canopied altar-tomb, c.1500, with C18 inscription to John Freke, surgeon, and his wife

Summary

St Bartholomew the Less is an interesting mixture of styles, with a complete contrast between the medieval tower and vestry and the unusual octagonal nave (compare St Dunstan in the West) with its Victorian and modern furnishings and windows.

The church is entered through the tower with its fine Gothic arches and then up several steps to the nave, which is at a higher level. The rib-vaulted ceiling is a beautiful feature and the modern stained glass east window includes the figures of St Bartholomew and Rahere.

The neighbouring Smithfield market was the scene of the famous meeting between Richard II and Wat Tyler, leader of the Peasants' revolt, in 1381. Tyler was taken into the hospital after being stabbed by Sir William Walworth, Lord Mayor, but was later dragged out and summarily beheaded.

Inigo Jones, the great architect, (buried in St Benet Paul's Wharf), was baptised here in 1573.

Situated inside the walls of London's oldest hospital, St Bartholomew the Less is unusual in having the hospital as its parish and it continues to provide a place of worship for patients, staff and visitors.

St Benet Paul's Wharf
Queen Victoria Street

History

- Named after St Benedict ("St Benet"), founder of western monasticism, and the nearby wharf, owned by the Dean and Chapter of St Paul's Cathedral

- Rebuilt by Wren, 1678-84, with some evidence of involvement by Robert Hooke

- Given to the Welsh Episcopalian Church in 1879, when under threat of demolition. Today, it is the Metropolitan Welsh Church

- Escaped WW2 unscathed, but suffered fire damage to the east corner of the north gallery in 1971, caused by vandals

Exterior

- Dark red brick, with blue brick headers and stone dressings, including festoons over the round-headed windows and painted quoins on all corners

- Delightful tower, with lead dome, lantern and small spire

- Hipped roof on north side

Interior

- Small (51 x 41 feet) with large, plain glass windows and flat ceiling

- North aisle and gallery, supported on Corinthian columns, formerly used by the ecclesiastical lawyers of Doctors Commons and still used by the Heralds from the College of Arms. On the front of the gallery are the Royal Arms, with those of the Archbishop of Canterbury and the Court of Admiralty (fouled anchor) on either side

- West gallery carrying modern organ

- Fine Royal Arms of Charles II above door to tower vestibule
- Reredos featuring tetragrammaton (the Divine name in Hebrew characters)
- Magnificent communion table with carvings of angels on legs and figure of Charity on the stretcher
- Poor-box with twisted baluster legs
- Simple carved pulpit, the tester being on the ceiling in the vestibule, beneath the tower
- Memorial to Inigo Jones, buried in chancel of pre-Fire church

Summary

One of the most attractive and lovable of the City churches, St Benet may well owe its design to Hooke, who was certainly responsible for some of the drawings. Despite the building of a flyover right beside it, the church retains the charms that were more suitably displayed when its position was rather less exposed.

The red and blue brick exterior and the little steeple are quite delightful. The interior, so small, yet so full of light, has many excellent features, including a beautifully carved communion table. There is an unusual view to be had of the dome of St Paul's through the leaded light windows of the north gallery.

The church is mentioned by Shakespeare in Twelfth Night – *"the bells of St Bennet, sir, may put you in mind"* says the Clown. Threatened with demolition in the 19th century, we must be grateful to the Welsh Episcopalians to whom it was given in 1879 and who have kept it in use until the present day, with services still conducted in Welsh on Sundays.

Top: St Olave Hart Street, Bayninge monument **Above:** St Botolph Aldgate

Opposite top: St Mary Abchurch, painted dome **Middle left:** St Giles Cripplegate, statue of St Giles
Middle right: St Alban Wood Street, surviving tower **Bottom:** St Ethelburga, churchyard garden

Top: St Andrew by the Wardrobe **Above:** St James Garlickhythe

Opposite top: Temple Church **Bottom:** St Mary Aldermary

Top: St Mary Abchurch **Above:** St Helen Bishopsgate, Sir Thomas Gresham tomb-chest

Opposite top: St Benet, from St Paul's dome **Bottom left:** St Bride **Bottom right:** St Mary le Bow

Top: The dome of St Stephen Walbrook

Above: St Mary le Bow, from courtyard garden

Above right: St Margaret Pattens, tondo

Right: St Mary le Bow, doorway

- Stained glass transparency in east window by James Pearson, 1788, Agony in the Garden, after a design by Nathaniel Clarkson

- Four Victorian windows in north aisle, showing the life of Christ

- Modern glass in south aisle depicting scenes from the church's history

- Several fine monuments, notably (south-east corner) Anne Packington, 1563, Gothic altar-tomb with canopy and, at the back, brass groups of kneeling figures

Summary

One of the main attractions of this church is its setting in Postman's Park, with its many rare and interesting trees and plants and G. F. Watts' unusual memorial to ordinary people who died saving others. This consists of a Japanese-style loggia enclosing a wall of tiles, each one inscribed with details of an action of heroic self-sacrifice.

The church itself is plain, apart from the little wooden bell-turret and classical east wall. The interior comes as a surprise, the blue and white ceiling with plaster rosettes and the blue and gold east end apse immediately commanding the attention. There is an obvious influence from George Dance the Younger's All Hallows London Wall. The transparency in the window above the altar is most impressive, whilst, at the west end, the convex organ gallery is also an attractive feature.

A plaque on the churchyard gate records the event in a nearby meeting house in 1738, when John Wesley felt his heart "strangely warmed" and went on to lead the Wesleyan Revival Movement. More details of this event are to be found on a memorial outside the entrance to the nearby Museum of London.

St Botolph Aldgate

Aldgate High Street

History

- One of four churches (three surviving) dedicated to the C7 Saxon abbot who became the patron saint of travellers, all the churches being situated close to main gates in the old City wall

- Under the patronage of Holy Trinity Priory, whose canons conducted services until the dissolution of the priory in 1531

- Escaped the Great Fire but rebuilt by George Dance the Elder in 1741-44, with restoration by J. F. Bentley in 1888-95 and Rodney Tatchell in 1965-66

Exterior

- One of the few City churches aligned north-south, instead of the more usual east-west

- South tower with clock stage and obelisk spire

- Red brick walls with stone dressings and Venetian windows

Interior

- Entrance through octagonal baptistery with C18 font

- Nave with galleries on three sides, supported on Tuscan columns

- C19 decorated ceiling by Bentley, with plaster angels in high relief, holding shields

- 1676 Renatus Harris organ, restored 2006

- Fine reredos with batik hangings by Thetis Blacker, 1982

- Pulpit c.1745 with inlaid panels

- Pews with scrolled arms

- C18 gilt wrought iron communion rails with a winged angel on the gate

- Elaborate C17 woodcarving on east (ritual south) wall of King David surrounded by musical instruments, from St Mary Whitechapel (destroyed in WW2)

- North (ritual east) window by Charles Clutterbuck, c.1850, on theme of Rubens' "Descent from the Cross"

- Fine monuments in baptistery, including: Thomas Lord Darcy and Sir Nicholas Carew, c.1560-70, two Catholics executed by Henry VIII; Robert Dow, 1612, wearing a Geneva cap and holding a skull; Sir John Cass, modern bust of the founder of the nearby school named after him

Summary

The original church of St Botolph stood just outside the historic Aldgate, through which travellers left the City to journey east. Chaucer lived in rooms above the gate in the late 14th century and the mighty Holy Trinity Priory stood just inside the City wall, until it became the first victim of Henry VIII's dissolution of the monasteries. Daniel Defoe was married in the church and left a harrowing account of the Great Plague of 1665, when over 5000 victims were buried in plague pits in the churchyard.

The present church was built by George Dance, architect of the Mansion House, and restored by J. F. Bentley, architect of Westminster Cathedral. Although Bentley's late 19th century restoration may not have been entirely in keeping with Dance's original intentions, the interior of the church has many interesting features, notably the superb woodcarving of King David surrounded by musical instruments and the colourful monument to Robert Dow.

St Botolph Bishopsgate

Bishopsgate

History

- One of four City churches (three surviving) dedicated to the C7 Saxon abbot, patron saint of travellers, because of their position close to main gates in the old City wall

- Survived the Great Fire, but rebuilt by James Gould in 1725-28

- Restorations in 1947-48 after WW2 bomb damage and in 1993-95 after the IRA Bishopsgate bomb

Exterior

- Stone-faced tower, unusually situated at the east end facing Bishopsgate, with a three-faced clock and crowned with a circular cupola, ogee cap and urn

- Red brick walls with stone dressings and windows in two tiers

- Churchyard to the south, made into a garden in 1863

- Parish hall to the west, built as an infants' school in 1861, with niches for Coade stone statues of two charity children, now kept inside

Interior

- Barrel-vaulted nave supported by massive Corinthian columns with galleries on three sides and a drum-shaped dome with lantern, inserted in the nave in an 1821 restoration

- Original pulpit, hexagonal and inlaid, with fine balusters

- Late C19 lectern and stalls by J. F. Bentley

- Original font from 1720s

- Fine gilded wrought iron sword-rest

- Organ of 1764, divided either side of west window in 1893

- Stained glass east window of the Crucifixion designed by F. W. Moody and made by Powell and Sons in 1869

- Monument on north-east gallery stairs to Sir Paul Pindar, 1650, owner of the C17 house in Bishopsgate, the façade of which is now in the Victoria and Albert Museum

Summary

Often called St Botolph without Bishopsgate, this church has stood, probably since Saxon times, just outside the old London wall. It was traditionally one of the richest parishes in the City and the church was rebuilt at substantial expense in the 1720s, after surviving the Great Fire. Its famous connections include Edward Alleyn, founder of Dulwich College, who was baptised here in 1566, and John Keats, baptised here in 1795.

This is the only City church with a tower at the east end above the chancel. The interior is a classic basilica in style, with aisles, galleries and a great barrel-vault. At the foot of the galleries are panels recording the names of all the rectors since 1323. The church has benefited from the increase in light created by the 19th century introduction of a dome in the centre of the nave.

The churchyard was the first in the City to be converted into a garden, back in 1863, which gives the building spacious surroundings. With netball courts also provided, it offers City workers a place for recreation as well as relaxation.

St Bride Fleet Street

Off Fleet Street

History

- The name St Bride is a corruption of St Bridget, a C5 Irish nun who, among other miracles, was said to have changed well-water into beer

- The church has Saxon origins and a long association with printing and the newspaper industry.

- Rebuilt by Wren, 1671-78, but with many C19 restorations

- Gutted by incendiary bombs in WW2 and restored by Godfrey Allen in 1955-57

Exterior

- Set in a high churchyard just off Fleet Street and hemmed in by buildings

- Wren's tallest steeple, 226ft high, consisting of five octagonal stages of diminishing sizes, the top stage being an obelisk spire

- Stone walls with round-headed aisle windows and oval clerestory windows

Interior

- Barrel-vaulted, aisled nave supported on double Tuscan columns, originally with galleries, which were replaced in Allen's post-war restoration by stalls, aligned east-west in college chapel style

- Large, plain glass windows giving great amounts of light to the interior

- Unusually high, free-standing reredos with stained glass central panel and trompe-l'oeil painting above by Glyn Jones, creating the illusion of an apse, also the illusion of statues of Moses and Aaron

- Large statues of St Bridget and St Paul, by David McFall, at west end

- Royal Arms, carved in stone by Kenneth Gardner

- Early C18 sculptures of two charity children by the font, originally from the St Bride and Bridewell schools in Bride Lane

- Extensive crypt, entered from north-west corner, featuring many impressive Roman, Saxon, Norman and medieval remains, together with an exhibition describing the history of St Bride and the development of the newspaper industry in Fleet Street

Summary

Known as "the Journalists' Church", St Bride has been associated with the printing business ever since Wynkyn de Worde brought his press to Fleet Street 500 years ago. During this time, the church has been connected to many of the most famous literary figures in history, including Shakespeare, Johnson, Boswell, Dryden, Evelyn, Milton, Keats and Dickens, as well as Samuel Pepys, who was baptised here.

Post-war excavations revealed the foundations of several earlier churches, as well as the remains of a significant Roman villa and many other relics from Saxon through to medieval times.

The church today is hidden away in narrow streets behind Fleet Street, but the glorious steeple can be seen from far away. One of Wren's best-loved creations, it was used by a local 18th century pastry chef, William Rich, as a model for a wedding cake, a design now common all over the world.

St Bride was the first of Wren's great basilica designs and the post-war restoration recreates much of the Wren interior, although the modern furnishings have an effect that is rather different from the architect's original intentions.

History

- One of two churches, at opposite ends of the City, dedicated to this saint, a Saxon Abbot of Glastonbury and Archbishop of Canterbury

- The medieval church survived the Great Fire, but was rebuilt in 1830-33 by John Shaw and his son, also John, on a site just north of the original, to allow road widening

- Some damage in WW2, restored in 1950

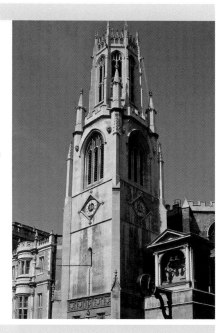

Exterior

- An octagonal building, aligned on a north-south axis, with square tower and tall, octagonal lantern

- Magnificent projecting clock, by Thomas Harris, 1671, returned to the church by Lord Rothermere in 1935 from St Dunstan's Lodge in Regent's Park, former home of Lord Hertford, who removed it when the old church was demolished in 1828

- Classical wooden aedicule above the clock, formerly on Ludgate (dem. 1760), housing figures of two giants, who strike the bells and turn their heads at each quarter hour

- Statue of Queen Elizabeth I, 1586, above statues of King Lud and his two sons in the vestry porch, all from the west wall of the old Ludgate

Interior

- An octagon with clerestory and star-ribbed vault

- Seven recesses, the altar being in the north and a C19 iconostasis (icon screen), brought from Antim monastery, Bucharest, screening off the north-west Romanian chapel. Altars in other recesses dedicated to different East European churches

- Altar and reredos, incorporating early C16 Flemish flamboyant carved woodwork

- Pulpit and box pews from 1830-33

- Modern stained glass in north (ritual east) window, with tracery lights from original window of 1830s

- Stained glass memorial to Isaak Walton, author of The Compleat Angler, in north-west window, behind the iconostasis

Summary

St Dunstan in the West is a distinctive church close to the western boundary of the City. Rebuilt in the 1830s, it is different in concept from any other church in the City, the octagonal lantern being modelled on All Saints Pavement, York.

In addition to the lantern, the exterior has several interesting features, including the 1586 statue of Queen Elizabeth and the famous clock, brought back to the church in 1935 after over 100 years in Regent's Park and said to be the first church clock in the City to have a minute hand.

Inside the church, there are strong connections with Eastern Europe, the elaborate Romanian iconostasis being a prominent feature. The rib-vaulted ceiling to the octagonal nave is also of outstanding beauty (compare St Bartholomew the Less).

The church has many interesting associations. Isaak Walton held the offices of "Scavenger, Quistman and Sidesman" from 1629-44, William Tyndale, Bible translator, was a preacher here in 1523, John Donne was rector, 1624-31, and St Dunstan's eight bells were the chimes of Dickens' Christmas Carol.

St Edmund King and Martyr

Lombard Street

History

- Dedicated to the young King of East Anglia, martyred by the Danish invaders in AD 870 (the Abbey of Bury St Edmunds being built on his burial place)

- First mentioned C12 as St Edmund Grasschurch, after the local hay market which gave its name to Gracechurch Street

- Rebuilt by Wren's office, 1670-74, possibly to a design by Robert Hooke

- Unusually, some bomb damage in WW1 and again in WW2, with subsequent restoration

Exterior

- Aligned on a north-south axis (cf. St Botolph Aldgate and St Dunstan in the West)

- Tower in centre of narrow south wall, with three bay façade and windows with cherub head keystones

- Steeple consisting of octagonal leaded lantern and trumpet-shaped spire

- Projecting clock of c.1810

Interior

- A plain rectangle, without aisles. Flat ceiling and small, projecting chancel, raised in a C19 restoration

- Reredos with carved panels and paintings of Moses and Aaron by William Etty, 1833

- Wren-period communion table and communion rails with elaborately carved balusters

- Finely carved pulpit, without tester

- Two organ cases, one of 1701-2 above the entrance, the other a replica of 1880, near the pulpit

- Two carved doorcases either side of reredos

- Fine marble font with cover featuring gilded figures of four of the apostles, set within semi-circular wooden railings with twisted balusters

44

- Late C17 Royal Arms, from St Dionis Backchurch (dem. 1878)

- Victorian stained glass in north (ritual east) window, "Christ in Glory"

Summary

St Edmund the King (as it is commonly known) is the only remaining church in Lombard Street, the historic centre of the banking industry, named after the Italians from Lombardy who first worked here. The street is famous for its hanging signs, representing the institutions which were based here. Many still hang over the street and St Edmund's projecting clock makes an interesting contrast.

The design of the south front is quite distinctive and the church can be clearly seen from Clement's Lane and also from the east side where it stands on George Yard. There is a small churchyard garden at the rear.

The church has been restored and refurbished and was re-opened in 2006 as home to the London Centre for Spirituality, whose bookshop is located in the nave. The church retains a number of fine Wren-period furnishings.

Among the church's associations are Joseph Addison, the poet and essayist, who was married here in 1716 and Rev Studdert Kennedy, a former rector, known as an army chaplain in the First World War by the nickname of "Woodbine Willie".

History

- Believed to be the only church in the country dedicated to St Ethelburga the Virgin, the C7 Saxon Abbess of the nunnery at Barking

- First mentioned in 1250 with parts of present building dating from 1390

- Restorations in 1861-62 and in early C20, with delicate chancel screen and west organ gallery by Sir Ninian Comper, 1912

- Partially hidden behind small shops on Bishopsgate until 1932

- Escaped damage in the Great Fire and in WW2

- Severely damaged by IRA Bishopsgate bomb in 1993

- Rebuilt to the designs of architects Purcell Miller Tritton and reopened as a Centre for Reconciliation and Peace in November 2002

Exterior

- Sandwiched between two large buildings on Bishopsgate

- Rebuilt west front, using fragments of the old wall, recreating the C14 doorway and three-light C15 window

- Mostly original square timber bell-turret of 1775 (only 30% damaged by the bomb), topped by 1671 weathercock, which survived intact

- Small, attractive walled garden at rear, with square raised pond and flowerbeds. Additional garden in Andalucian style added behind this in 2006, featuring Bedouin-style tent

Interior

- One of the smallest of the City churches, only 55ft long

- Plain rectangular nave with clerestory and south aisle, separated from the nave by original four-bay arcade

- C18 Gothic stone font, inscribed with Greek palindrome ("Cleanse my sins, not only my face") also on the font at St Martin Ludgate

- Stone slab near entrance with inscription "Bona intra, melior exi" ("Come in good, go out better")

- New altar and lectern by Julian Humphreys from timbers recovered from the bombsite

- Stained glass east window by Helen Whittaker, a student at the Prince's Foundation in Shoreditch, using fragments of glass from Kempe's 1878 window, destroyed in the bombing. The subject is St Ethelburga, shown collecting fragments of glass

Summary

For many years, St Ethelburga had been a rare survivor and reminder of what the City's small medieval churches had looked like. Squeezed in between modern buildings and, until they were demolished in 1932, set behind some little shops facing on to Bishopsgate, the church had serviced one of the smallest parishes in the City.

This all changed with the IRA bomb of 24th April, 1993, which seemingly caused the almost complete destruction of the church. Mercifully, the south arcade, along with the south and east walls and a few of the furnishings, survived and it was eventually decided to rebuild the church. It was reopened in 2002 as a Centre for Reconciliation and Peace.

St Giles Cripplegate

Barbican, off Fore Street

History

- Dedicated to St Giles, a C7 French hermit, who rescued a hind from hunting dogs, hence the frequent depiction of him with a deer.

- Cripplegate may refer to cripples or it may derive from the Saxon word "crepel", meaning a covered passage, which could have linked the City wall with a nearby barbican, or watch tower

- First mentioned in c.1100, rebuilt in 1390, with major restoration in mid-C16. Escaped the Great Fire but restored again in C19 and by Godfrey Allen after severe damage in WW2

Exterior

- Formerly surrounded by houses, but now isolated in the middle of the Barbican estate, standing in a paved area, on which are C19 gas lamps originally on Tower Bridge

- Gothic tower, with top stage heightened in 1682-84 and post-war wooden cupola

- Walls refaced in late C19, but with substantial C14 fabric remaining

Interior

- Late Perpendicular style with north and south aisles separated from the nave by an arcade of seven bays

- Sanctuary with stone arches and blue panelled roof with bosses. On the south side, medieval piscina and sedilia, with tiles of Roman origin

- Post-war west gallery with C18 organ from St Luke Old Street

- Pews and altar from St Luke, also the elegant font and domed cover

- Flamboyant modern sword-rest, replacing one destroyed in WW2, showing coats-of-arms of six Lord Mayors

- Modern stained glass windows, the east depicting various religious figures with connections to the church, the north a tribute to Edward Alleyn, parishioner and founder of Dulwich College

- Monuments (south aisle): John Speed, 1629, historian and mapmaker, holding book and skull; bust of John Milton by John Bacon; plaque in memory of Sir Martin Frobisher, Elizabethan sailor and explorer; 1904 bronze statue of Milton

- Busts, c.1900, of Milton, Defoe, Cromwell and Bunyan

Summary

Although much restored, St Giles is a survivor of the mid-16th century late Perpendicular style of church-building. Today, it stands somewhat isolated, beside a lake in the middle of the Barbican development.

St Giles is situated just outside the old City wall, fragments of which can be seen nearby. It is rich in historical associations. Milton was buried here in 1674 and his grave is marked by a stone in the chancel floor. Shakespeare attended his nephew's baptism in the church in 1607, Defoe was born in the neighbouring Fore Street and Bunyan attended and preached here.

Lancelot Andrewes, the Anglican Divine and Bible translator, became vicar of St Giles in 1588, the year when Sir Martin Frobisher, later buried here, was helping to defeat the Spanish Armada. Oliver Cromwell was married in the church in 1620 and William Holman Hunt, pre-Raphaelite painter, baptised here in 1827

St Helen Bishopsgate
Great St Helen's, off Bishopsgate

History

- Dedicated to the mother of Constantine, the first Christian Emperor of Rome

- The church consists of two halves, the nun's church of an early C13 Benedictine nunnery being built alongside the existing parish church

- Nunnery suppressed in 1538, but both churches survived the Great Fire and WW2

- Major interior restorations by the Victorians and by Quinlan Terry in 1993-95

Exterior

- Charming west front, with embattled gables and wooden bell turret

- Two doors through which to enter the unusual double nave, the C16 door into the former nuns' church on the left and the C14 door into the former parish church on the right.

- Other walls containing fabric from C12 to C16

Interior

- Four-bay arcade between north and south naves dating from late C15, with chancels separated by two arches of early C14 (west) and early C15 (east)

- Raised floor, introduced by Terry, at a uniform height throughout

- C14 niches and two C14 piscinae on east wall of south transept

- Nun's squint at bottom of north-east wall

- J. L. Pearson's former chancel screen of 1892-93 now positioned across the south transept

- West gallery by Terry, with modern organ in C18 case

- Richly decorated pulpit of 1633 on south wall

- Two sword-rests, one of wrought iron, one, very rare, of wood, dated 1665

- Poor-box on wooden figure of a bearded beggar, early C17

- Magnificent collection of monuments, including: (north wall, above gallery) Alderman Robinson, 1599; (north wall) Martin Bond, 1643, in military uniform, surrounded by figures in Civil War dress, William Bond, 1576, and family; (north-east floor) Sir Thomas Gresham, 1579, marble tomb-chest; (beneath chancel arches) Sir William Pickering, 1574, six-poster monument with iron rails; (between chancel and south transept) Sir John Crosby, 1476, and wife, alabaster figures on tomb-chest, Sir John de Oteswich and wife, late C14, also alabaster figures on tomb-chest; (south wall) Richard Staper, 1608, kneeling figures, Lord Mayor Sir John Spencer, 1609 and wife, very large and elaborate wall monument and tomb-chest, with daughter kneeling at prayer

Summary

A splendid reminder of medieval times, St Helen Bishopsgate has many original features from the 13th and 14th centuries, including a nun's squint, or hagioscope, through which the church altar could be viewed from the nunnery.

The church was heavily Victorianised and another major restoration was undertaken in the 1990s, when the floor was raised by several feet, leaving the piers unduly shortened and some of the wall monuments standing below floor level.

The historic exterior of the church has survived and the collection of splendid monuments, unequalled in any City church, testifies to the wealth of the Bishopsgate area, where many of London's most prominent businessmen lived and worshipped.

St James Garlickhythe

Upper Thames Street

History

- Named after St James, the Apostle, who died in Spain, where his bones were apparently discovered 800 years later in Compostela. Pilgrims to the site took away sea shells, which became the saint's symbol

- Garlickhythe refers to the nearby wharf where garlic was brought into the City

- Rebuilt by Wren in 1676-82

- Some damage from a bomb in 1917 and a lucky escape in 1940 when a 500 pounder landed in the south-east corner but failed to explode

- Significant damage to roof, south wall and window, plus pews, caused by a crane falling from across the street in 1991

Exterior

- Plain west tower with steeple of three square stages, recessed behind a pierced parapet, the lowest stage with pairs of diagonally projecting columns on each corner. Similar to those at St Michael Paternoster Royal and St Stephen Walbrook

- Charming figure of St James standing on a projecting clock (a 1988 replica of the original) with sea shell beneath

Interior

- Wren's highest church interior, with additional clerestory level, the ceiling painted with blue sky and clouds

- Projecting chancel, with painting of the Ascension by Andrew Geddes (1815) which replaced the east window, blocked in to strengthen the walls

- Fine pulpit, with wig peg(!) and choir stalls, all from St Michael Queenhythe (dem. 1876)

- Pews made from oak trees blown down on a Sussex estate in the hurricane of 1987, replacing those destroyed in 1991

- Small tables on either side of altar made from wood from the Marchioness pleasure boat, which sank in 1989 with the loss of many young people's lives

- West gallery with magnificent Father Smith organ

- Modern bust of Thomas Cranmer, 1989

- Two wrought iron sword-rests, one from St Michael Queenhythe

Summary

Often called "Wren's Lantern" on account of the light that pours into the high interior of this church from the clerestory windows, St James Garlickhythe stands prominently on Upper Thames Street, although, before the road was widened, it was surrounded by buildings and much less exposed.

The church has a fine interior, although the grey painted panelling and the ceiling with its blue sky and clouds are not ideally suited to a Wren church. The woodwork is outstanding, in particular the pulpit, tester and choir stalls with their twisted balusters. There are some delightful trumpeting angels on top of the organ and St James's shell is prominent in several places.

In the vestibule and behind the pulpit are some interesting photographs and paintings of the church in past times, which remind us that this is another historic Wren church that has survived remarkably well.

St Katharine Cree

Leadenhall Street

History

- Originally built in the grounds of Holy Trinity Priory in c.1280 to provide a lay church which would not interfere with the devotions of the canons in the Augustinian monastery

- "Cree" is a corruption of "Christ"(church), a reference to the priory

- Rebuilt in 1628 and consecrated by Archbishop Laud in 1631

- Escaped serious damage in both the Great Fire and WW2

Exterior

- Medieval tower (c.1500) with cupola of 1776

- Five square-headed windows on south side, with Gothic tracery

- Unusually delicate sundial of 1706 in middle of south wall

- Churchyard (entered from Mitre Street) with 1631 Avenon gateway, built by William Avenon and formerly on Leadenhall Street, with a memorial to James Fitch, who set up a cheesemonger's shop nearby in 1784

Interior

- Six bays with Corinthian columns and clerestory above

- Intricate Gothic ceiling with 17 coloured bosses featuring coats-of-arms of the City and various Livery Companies

- Original 1630 east window in shape of St. Katharine's wheel

- 1686 Father Smith organ with beautifully carved case, a major restoration having been completed in 2006

- Reredos from St James Duke's Place (dem. 1874)

- Finely carved pulpit with hexagonal tester inlaid with seven different woods

- C17 octagonal alabaster font with ogee-domed cover, given by Lord Mayor Sir John Gayer

- Laud Memorial Chapel in south-east, with elaborate monument to Sir Nicholas Throckmorton, Elizabethan statesman and Ambassador to France

- Wooden statue of King Charles I in the nave
- Memorial window and plaque in south aisle to SS Lancastria, which was sunk in 1940 with loss of 4000 lives

Summary

St Katharine Cree is a most unusual church, being a very rare example of early 17th century church-building in the City and representing a period when the Gothic style was giving way to the Classical.

Externally, the little tower of c.1500 contrasts with the body of the church, which has square-headed windows, but with Gothic tracery. The interior is dominated by a truly beautiful Gothic ribbed ceiling. The east window, in the shape of St Katharine's wheel, is also Gothic and again contrasts with the classical Corinthian columns in the nave. Regrettably, the overall appearance is marred by the boxing-in of the aisles for offices, although it seems that there may be plans to remove these at some stage.

On the 16th October each year, the Lion Sermon is given, a tradition introduced by Lord Mayor Sir John Gayer in thanks for being spared when he encountered a lion whilst on a journey through Syria in 1643. The church also has strong connections with Archbishop Laud, a close confidant of King Charles I. Laud was executed in 1645 for his High Church views and persecution of Puritans.

History

- Dedicated to St Lawrence, who was martyred by slow-roasting on a gridiron. "Jewry" refers to the church's position on the edge of the Jewish quarter of the medieval City

- Rebuilt by Wren, 1671-77, gutted by bombs on 29 December 1940 and beautifully restored by Cecil Brown, 1954-7

- Official church of the City of London Corporation

Exterior

- An irregular shape, reflecting the pre-Great Fire site, with the west wall out of true alignment and the steeple (a post-war fibre-glass replica) therefore appearing oddly out of line with the tower

- Weathervane in the shape of the saint's gridiron

- Classical east façade, featuring round-arched windows and niches and Corinthian columns and pilasters, supporting a pediment and attic storey

Interior

- Spacious hall-type interior with striking white and gilt ceiling

- Commonwealth Chapel on north-east side, with country flags and finely-carved oak screen, incorporating a wrought iron section given by the Royal Marines

• Large west organ gallery and tiny north trumpeter's gallery above fine vestry door

- Pews for Lord Mayor, sheriffs, aldermen and esquires

- Main pews from Holy Trinity, Marylebone

- 1620 font from Holy Trinity, Minories, the cover made of wood from the bombed Guildhall roof

- Eight chandeliers by Cecil Brown

- Steinway grand piano, formerly owned by Sir Thomas Beecham

- Stained glass windows by Christopher Webb, including: (east) the arms of Balliol College, Oxford and the Archbishop of Canterbury, former patrons of the church; (south-east) Sir Thomas More, who preached here; and (vestibule) Sir Christopher Wren, flanked by his master craftsmen Grinling Gibbons and Edward Strong, above outlines of the Wren City steeples and the dome of St Paul's

Summary

The official church of the City of London Corporation, St Lawrence Jewry stands proudly beside Guildhall Yard, on Gresham Street. Wren's classical east façade reflects the position of the church on the traditional route into the Guildhall.

Cecil Brown's rebuilding of the interior, after the church was gutted by incendiary bombs in the Second World War, is widely regarded as one of the best of the City church restorations. The white and gold of the ceiling and the chandeliers create a striking impression and there is also some excellent modern woodwork to admire, particularly the screen alongside the Commonwealth Chapel, built to commemorate the City's role in the development of the Commonwealth. The New Zealand Society celebrate their National Day here annually.

Although stained glass was never a feature of Wren's churches, Christopher Webb's work seems quite in keeping with the rest of the interior and contributes to the overall feeling of importance that this church imparts.

History

- Traditionally thought to be dedicated to a Norwegian King of the Orkneys, killed in 1116, but possibly named after a C3 martyr

- Situated at north end of old London Bridge (moved upstream in 1831)

- Close to source of the Great Fire and therefore one of the first churches to burn down. Rebuilt by Wren in 1671-84, taking over work started by the parish

- Many subsequent restorations, though very little damage in WW2

Exterior

- Set beside the river behind a well laid out garden, but overshadowed on the west by the 1920s neo-Egyptian Adelaide House

- One of Wren's most famous steeples, the tower surmounted by a large arcaded stone octagon, lead-covered dome, small lantern and obelisk spire, probably influenced by the similar design at St Charles Borromeo, Antwerp

- Arch beneath tower created in 1760s to provide footpath for pedestrians, after widening of road from London Bridge

- Fine projecting clock, provided by Lord Mayor Sir Charles Duncombe in 1709

- Portland stone walls, with large windows on the north side reduced to small circular ones to reduce late C18 traffic noise and east window blocked in to cut out the "foul language" from Billingsgate market

Interior

- Barrel-vaulted ceiling with oval clerestory windows and aisles separated from nave by Ionic columns

- Two-storey reredos with carved pelican in piety, paintings of Moses and Aaron and a painted glory

- Wren-period pulpit by William Grey, with large, beautifully carved tester

- Magnificent west gallery and organ-case, reached from the vestibule by double staircases with twisted balusters

- Vestibule screen with fine octagonal glazing

- Churchwardens' pews at west end of nave

- C17 font with octagonal gadrooned bowl and finely-carved cover

- Fine wrought iron sword-rest of 1708

- C19 Russian icon (north wall)

- 1924 statue of St Magnus (south wall)

Summary

St Magnus has suffered from so many major alterations from the 17th through to the 20th century, that it is difficult to imagine what it was like in Wren's time, apart from the steeple, of course, which is still a wonderful sight, though much obscured by other buildings.

The interior, very High Church in style, particularly since the restoration work of Martin Travers in 1924-25, has some of the finest woodwork in the City. The lofty nave and Ionic columns are a reminder of the words of T. S. Eliot in The Wasteland, *"where the walls of Magnus Martyr hold inexplicable splendour of Ionian white and gold"*

Perhaps the most famous association of the church is with its 16th century rector, Miles Coverdale, who, with William Tyndale, published the first Bible in the English language and whose body is buried here.

History

- Named after the Maid of Antioch, who died for her Christian beliefs and Lothbury, the street in which the church stands

- Rebuilt by Wren, 1686-90, the church today incorporates the parishes of seven other churches lost between the time of the Great Fire and WW2

- One of the few City churches to escape damage in WW2

Exterior

- Portland stone tower on south-west corner, with lead obelisk spire on a bell-shaped dome

- South wall on Lothbury, with three round-headed windows between a vestry window and an elegant classical doorcase in the tower

Interior

- Irregular shaped interior, the east wall being at an angle to the other walls

- Nave and south aisle, the latter made into a separate chapel by Corinthian columns and a wooden screen partially made from the communion rails of St Olave Jewry (dem. 1888)

- Organ on small west gallery

- Ornate chancel screen from All Hallows the Great (dem. 1894), with fine twisted balusters and William and Mary's Royal Arms in a broken pediment above a large eagle

- Magnificent reredos flanked by paintings of Moses and Aaron from St Christopher le Stocks (dem. 1781)

- Finely carved pulpit and tester, the latter from All Hallows the Great

- Two C18 candelabra in the sanctuary, both from All Hallows the Great, with modern copies in the nave

- Smaller reredos in south aisle from St Olave Jewry

- Exceptionally fine font (south aisle) from St Olave Jewry, with carvings of Adam and Eve, Noah's Ark, the Baptism of Christ and the Baptism of the Eunuch, between cherub heads

- Fine busts (south aisle) of Alderman John Boydell (Lord Mayor 1790), from St Olave Jewry, and of Mrs Ann Simpson

Summary

St Margaret Lothbury is easy to overlook, tucked away as it is behind the Bank of England. Its Portland stone exterior and slender, lead-covered steeple are reminiscent of other Wren churches, such as St Martin Ludgate and St Augustine.

The attraction of the church lies chiefly in its interior, featuring many exceptional furnishings from other City churches, particularly All Hallows the Great and St Olave Jewry, both demolished in the 19th century. Most notable among these are the magnificent Wren-period wooden chancel screen, one of only two in the City (the other being in St Peter Cornhill), and the superb carved font in the south aisle, surely among the best to be seen anywhere.

Having escaped damage in the War, St Margaret Lothbury can offer the visitor a collection of fine original 17th century features, albeit that many originated in churches other than St Margaret itself.

St Margaret Pattens

Eastcheap

History

- Dedicated to the Maid of Antioch, a Christian martyr. "Pattens" may refer to the wooden soles raised on iron hoops to keep women's shoes above the dirty streets, which were made in the neighbourhood.

- Rebuilt by Wren, 1684-87

- Some Victorian restoration, plus repairs in the 1950s to WW2 bomb damage

Exterior

- Elegant 200ft high lead-covered spire on a tower with four corner pinnacles

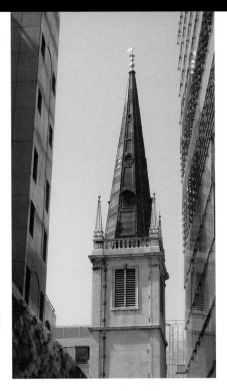

- Set on the corner of Rood Lane and separated from Eastcheap by some attractive early C18 shops

Interior

- Rectangular, with north aisle/Lady Chapel and gallery (converted into offices during 1950s restoration), also organ gallery at west end

- Rare canopied churchwardens' pews (west end)

- Fine Wren-period reredos, with painting by Carlo Maratta of Christ in the Garden of Gethsemane

- Beadle's pew in north-east corner

- Hexagonal pulpit with iron hour-glass stand

- Copper cross on south wall, taken down from top of spire for safety

- Below it, a wooden memorial board to King Charles I, installed by pro-Jacobite rector of late C19, Rev James Fish

- Large tablet on south floor to James Donaldson, the City Garbler, responsible for selecting spices for the City

- Tondo, attributed to Della Robbia, in north aisle reredos

- Memorial in north aisle to crew of submarine K4, sunk in 1918
- Royal Arms of James II above west door
- Lectern with an eagle holding a viper in its claws
- Two sword-rests, one of pole and one of frame design

Summary

Best seen from beneath the clock on the east wall of St Mary at Hill, the elegant lead-covered spire of St Margaret Pattens is the only surviving true spire built by Wren. (There were originally two others, St Antholin, which was demolished in 1875, and St Swithin, destroyed in the Second World War).

The church has a spacious interior, with many interesting features, particularly the magnificent churchwardens' pews, the row of wig-pegs in the north aisle and the very fine tondo, attributed to Della Robbia, the 15th century Italian sculptor.

A pair of original pattens is still in safekeeping in the vestry, along with the hour-glass formerly used for timing the sermon (29 minutes apparently being the limit before the sand ran out!)

Although the church is hemmed in on one side by the massive glass structure of Plantation Place, a fine reflection of the spire can be seen in the glass frontage of a building in Fenchurch Street, directly opposite the top of Rood Lane.

St Martin Ludgate

Ludgate Hill

History

- Dedicated to a Roman soldier who, in bitter weather, gave half his cloak to a beggar and who went on to become Bishop of Tours. The church, often titled "within" Ludgate, stood just inside this historic entrance into the City

- Rebuilt by Wren, 1677-86, with the substantial involvement of Robert Hooke.

- One of the few City churches to escape any damage in WW2

Exterior

- Portland stone tower in centre of south front, with scrolled volutes to the upper stage, upon which is a delightful lead steeple, comprising ogee dome, balcony, lantern and obelisk spire.

- Brick north wall, facing on to Stationers' Hall garden

Interior

- The church has a longer north-south axis than east-west, but the interior is squared off by the creation of an entrance vestibule with gallery above, allowing the altar to be set conventionally in the east and, at the same time, insulating the nave from outside traffic noise

- Greek cross-in-a-square design (cf. St Anne and St Agnes and St Mary at Hill), with barrel-vaulted arms meeting in a groin-vaulted centre supported by four Corinthian columns

- South gallery separated from the nave by coffered arches. Three fine carved doorcases below, all by William Emmett, (the one in the south-east often wrongly attributed to Grinling Gibbons)

- Beneath the west organ gallery, a C17 marble font inscribed with a Greek palindrome ("Cleanse my sins, not only my face" – cf. St Ethelburga) with a carved marble pelican in piety behind

- Central chandelier from St Vincent Cathedral, West Indies

- Original reredos, communion table, communion rails and pulpit

- 1720 painting of the Ascension by R. Browne to north of altar, from St Mary Magdalen (dem. 1893)

- Double churchwardens' chair, 1690, unique in the City

- C18 sword-rest from St Mary Magdalen

- Bread shelves for the poor, from St Mary Magdalen

Summary

A relatively unaltered Wren church and one of very few to survive the Second World War intact, St Martin's delicate steeple can still be clearly seen above the City skyline, as the architect intended. Viewed from a certain point along Fleet Street, the spire perfectly bisects the dome of St Paul's.

Working in Wren's office, it appears that Hooke had a key role in the building of this church, for he is known to have visited it more than thirty times during its construction.

The interior, with its ingenious solution to the problem created by the north-south oblong shape, has some fine original woodwork. Although the unimpressive Victorian stained glass makes the church rather darker than it should be, St Martin Ludgate remains one of the most original of the surviving Wren churches.

St Mary Abchurch

Abchurch Lane, off Cannon Street

History

- Possibly named after a benefactor called Abba, or a corruption of "Up" church (i.e. up the hill from the river)

- First mentioned in C12, rebuilt after the Great Fire by Wren, 1681-86

- Some bomb damage in WW2, skilfully restored by Godfrey Allen

Exterior

- Situated in a paved courtyard on a narrow side-street

- Dark red brick walls, with stone quoins and dressings

- Steeple consisting of ogee-domed base, small pierced lantern and obelisk spire

Interior

- Painted dome (unique in a City church) by parishioner William Snow, 1708, featuring the Divine name in Hebrew characters (the tetragrammaton), surrounded by a glory, a chorus of worshipping cherubs and angels and, below, figures representing the Christian virtues

- Large reredos by Grinling Gibbons (authenticated by written requests for payment of £30 for the work). Exquisite limewood carvings of fruit and flowers and, in the centre, a gilded pelican in piety

- Pulpit and tester of outstanding merit by William Grey, with fine twisted balusters

- North and south doorcases of exceptional quality by William Emmett. Copper pelican in piety on north doorcase, formerly the weathervane, removed for safety reasons in 1764

- Royal Arms of James II, also by Emmett, above west vestry door

- Font by William Kempster, with unusually fine cover like a small pavilion, featuring Emmett's carvings of the four evangelists

- Original box pews on north, west and south sides, one with a dog kennel below until its removal in 1946

- Organ by Noel Mander, 1954, with organ-case of 1717, originally from All Hallows, Bread Street, set on west gallery

- Fine monument to Sir Patience Ward (Lord Mayor 1680-81) to south of reredos

- Original poor-boxes on either side of west vestry door, with beadle's seat next to the one on the south side

Summary

The exterior of this little masterpiece gives no hint of the treasures that lie within. Wren shows his genius by creating an illusion of space in an area just 63 feet by 60 feet, through the expedient of a dome, 40 feet in diameter, supported on the walls of the building, without additional buttressing.

The reredos, one of only two authenticated examples of the work of Grinling Gibbons in a City church, (the other being the font cover in All Hallows by the Tower), is of outstanding quality and was superbly repaired after falling from the wall when a Second World War bomb exploded nearby, breaking it into some 2,000 pieces. The rest of the woodwork is also quite exceptional, notably the pulpit and tester, doorcases, royal coat of arms and font cover.

We are indeed fortunate that this little church has come down to us almost entirely unaltered, as an example of the workmanship of Wren and his finest craftsmen.

History

- First mentioned in 1177, rebuilt by Wren, 1670-74, re-using much medieval fabric which survived the Great Fire

- Restoration by George Gwilt in late C18, including rebuilding of west tower

- Further restorations in first half of C19, also in the late 1960s and after a serious fire in 1988

Exterior

- Dark, red brick, battlemented west tower on Lovat Lane

- Yellow brick south side, facing the narrow Church Passage

- Classical east front, facing St Mary at Hill (the street), with fine Venetian window and projecting clock

- Churchyard on north side, entered from St Mary at Hill, with yellow brick north wall

Interior

- Greek cross-in-a-square design, with four equal arms meeting at a shallow central dome, supported on four free-standing columns (a Byzantine "quincunx" plan)

- West gallery and screen by the talented Victorian woodcarver, William Gibbs Rogers, in the style of Grinling Gibbons

- Original box pews, plus fine reredos, pulpit and other woodwork, much of it by Gibbs Rogers, are in storage, following the fire of 1988, awaiting full restoration

- Six fine sword-rests also in storage

- Stone relief of the Resurrection, c.1600, on north wall of vestibule, originally above entrance to churchyard

Summary

Tucked away among streets and alleyways that have changed little since medieval times, St Mary at Hill is among the most attractive of the City churches, despite the absence of most of its furnishings, which have been in storage since the restoration of 1990-92 and which include much fine woodcarving.

There is a considerable amount of medieval stonework in the lower walls, which Wren built upon and which have seen several subsequent restorations. The result is a mixture of styles and influences which is quite fascinating.

One of the few churches to escape damage in the Second World War, St Mary at Hill suffered severely from a fire in 1988. The restoration of the interior is of exceptional quality and enables the visitor to admire the unusual design, in which four columns support a shallow saucer-dome in the centre of a Greek cross pattern of four equal arms. There are similarities here to the designs of St Anne and St Agnes and St Martin Ludgate, though those churches do not have the central dome.

There is an excellent view to be had of St Margaret Pattens church from beneath the clock which projects from the east wall of St Mary at Hill. A little further up the street is the entrance to the hidden churchyard from which one can gain access to the church through a fine entrance vestibule.

St Mary le Bow
Cheapside

History

- Probably named after the arches, or bows, in the Norman crypt beneath the church

- Referred to, from the 11th century onwards, as one of the City's most important churches, its bell rang the curfew at 9pm each evening from 1469 until the practice was discontinued in 1876

- Rebuilt in 1670-80 by Wren, who, in building the tower, discovered the Norman crypt and a Roman roadway below

- Gutted by incendiary bombs on 10th May, 1941 and restored by Laurence King, 1956-64

Exterior

- Wren's most celebrated steeple, on a square tower entered through two classical doorways, each set in a rusticated niche beneath a frieze of cherub heads and two carved angels

- Red brick west wall, with large round-headed window above the central door, flanked by two similar, but smaller, windows with circular windows above

- In the courtyard garden, a statue to Captain John Smith, leader of the first British overseas settlement, established in Jamestown, Virginia in 1607

Interior

- Almost square, 3-bay interior, with narrow aisles, modelled on the Basilica of Constantine and Maxentius in Rome

- Keystones carved with heads of those involved in the post-war restoration

- Barrel-vaulted ceiling, painted blue and white, with gold decorations

- Chancel divided from nave by a hanging rood, made in Oberammergau and a gift from the people of Germany

- Free-standing altar with Bishop's Throne nearby

- Twin pulpits to facilitate lunchtime debates

- Vibrant-coloured stained glass windows by John Hayward

Summary

The steeple of St Mary le Bow, one of Wren's greatest achievements, has dominated the skyline in Cheapside for the last 300 years. Wren takes our eyes up from the square tower and balustrade through a central rotunda of 12 elegant columns, a circular balustrade and then, via little flying buttresses, to another square stage with 12 small columns. On top of this is an obelisk spire, capped by a golden ball and a nine foot long copper dragon, flying serenely 224 feet above the streets of the City.

The church is also famous for the Bow bells, within sound of which all true Cockneys are born and which are said to have called Dick Whittington back to become Lord Mayor of London in 1397. The "great bell of Bow" features in the "Oranges and Lemons" nursery rhyme and was used to sound the curfew in the City.

The red brick west wall of the church has an inviting appearance when seen from the garden in front of it, but the post-war restoration of the interior is not in sympathy with Wren's ideals. The 11th century crypt below is, however, a remarkable survival from Norman times, part now fitted as a chapel and the remainder open on weekday lunchtimes as a vegetarian restaurant.

St Mary Woolnoth

Lombard Street/King William Street

History

- Possibly named after Wulfnoth, a suggested C11 founder of the church, or from the nearby wool market of the Middle Ages

- Partly restored after the Great Fire, then completely rebuilt by Nicholas Hawksmoor in 1716-27

- Substantial restoration by William Butterfield, 1875-76

- Saved from threatened demolition many times in the late C19/early C20, notably when the site was required by the City and South London Railway for the development of Bank station, subsequently built underneath the church

- Escaped unscathed from WW2

Exterior

- Prominently situated on the corner of Lombard Street and King William Street

- Powerful, fortress-like west front with banded rustication and Tuscan columns beneath an upper stage with Composite columns, topped by twin turrets, the whole tower being broader than it is deep

- North wall with three round-headed rusticated niches and projecting clock

Interior

- Square, centralised nave with four groups of three Corinthian columns carrying an entablature with large, semicircular clerestory windows above

- Wooden former gallery fronts set back against the walls in Butterfield's restoration

- West organ gallery with instrument said to be by Father Smith; second organ in north aisle

- Raised chancel, with coloured marble tiles by Butterfield

- Black and gold baldacchino above the altar, with twisted columns and elaborate canopy

- Bulging pulpit and large, square tester, the former lowered and the latter raised by Butterfield

Summary

Hawksmoor's only City church, St Mary Woolnoth is a highly original testament to the skills of Wren's talented pupil. The exterior gives a sense of awesome strength, whilst the interior is lofty and well-lit by fine clerestory windows.

St Mary Woolnoth has the unusual distinction of being the only City church to have beneath it an underground station, which, in works of 1897-1900, replaced the crypt, the bodies in the vault being removed to the City cemetery in Manor Park, Ilford. These included the remains of Edward Lloyd, owner of the nearby coffee-shop in which Lloyd's of London was founded.

Other associations include John Newton, a former minister here and composer of such hymns as "Amazing Grace", "How Sweet the Name of Jesus Sounds" and "Glorious Things of Thee are Spoken". T. S. Eliot worked in Lloyd's Bank just opposite the church in Lombard Street and wrote in The Wasteland:

> *"And each man fixed his eyes before his feet*
> *Flowed up the hill and down King William Street*
> *To where St Mary Woolnoth kept the hours*
> *With a dead sound on the final stroke of nine"*

History

- Built on the site of the Roman basilica, Cornhill being one of the two hills (the other being Ludgate) on which the Romans established Londinium after their arrival in AD 43

- One of the few City churches known to have been of Saxon foundation

- Rebuilt after the Great Fire by "skilful workmen" appointed by the parish

- Tower rebuilt in early C18, with Nicholas Hawksmoor responsible for the upper stages in 1718-22

- Completely remodelled and Victorianised by Sir George Gilbert Scott, 1857-60

Exterior

- Gothic tower with angle turrets and pinnacles

- Portland stone south wall, with round-headed windows, facing on to a churchyard garden set in a labyrinth of historic alleyways of the City

- Entrance through the tower, via Scott's elaborately carved Gothic porch with tympanum featuring a sculpture by J. Birnie Philip of "St Michael Disputing with Satan about the body of Moses"

- On right of the doorway, a war memorial in the form of a bronze statue of St Michael by Richard Goulden

Interior

- Nave, aisles and chancel in Victorian Gothic style, with Tuscan columns and blue-painted ceiling

- Stained glass south aisle windows with Lombard-style tracery and circular clerestory windows above

- Pink marble Italianate reredos by Scott

- Finely-carved pews, 1859-60, by William Gibbs Rogers, who was also responsible for the pulpit and lectern

- Octagonal font of 1672

- Renatus Harris organ of 1684, rebuilt on several occasions

- C18 wrought iron sword-rest
- Large carved wooden pelican in piety inside the entrance door, saved by the rector's daughter from intended destruction in Scott's restoration, it is said, by the payment of 2/6d to a workman

Summary

Although generally considered a "Wren church", it appears that Wren himself was not involved in the design of this building. In any case, little of the 17th century work is to be seen today, as the church was altered more than any other in the City by the Victorian restorers.

There are, nonetheless, a number of outstanding features to interest the visitor. The churchyard, hemmed in behind the buildings of Cornhill, has been turned into a delightful garden and is set beside the historic Jamaica Wine Lodge in a maze of alleyways of the old City. From this side, an excellent view can be had of Hawksmoor's Gothic tower.

Inside the church, there are good examples of the work of a fine 19th century woodcarver, William Gibbs Rogers. Of particular note are the pew bench-ends, one (south aisle) carved with the Scapegoat, after Holman Hunt's painting, and others featuring the Return from Egypt (south aisle), Charity protecting three children (north aisle) and a pelican (also north aisle).

St Michael Paternoster Royal

College Street, by Upper Thames Street

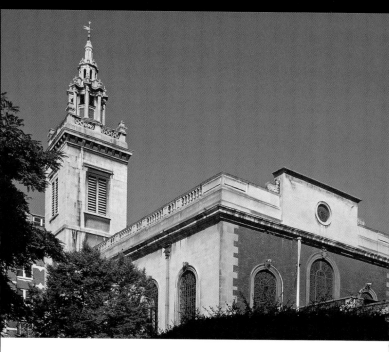

History

- Named Paternoster after the rosary makers in the neighbouring lane and Royal, a corruption of La Reole, a town in Bordeaux with a connection to the local wine importing district

- Famous as the church of Richard Whittington, four times Lord Mayor of London, who founded a College of Priests and an almshouse in College Hill and paid for the rebuilding of the church in 1409

- Rebuilt by Wren, 1685-94

- Restored in the C19 and again in the 1960s, by Elidir Davies, after being badly damaged by bombing in WW2

- Tower and west end now the headquarters of the Mission to Seafarers, a Church of England voluntary society which cares for seafarers of all nations

Exterior

- Delightful three-stage steeple in a similar style to those at St James Garlickhythe and St Stephen Walbrook, but octagonal rather than square, with eight columns at the angles.

- Stone-faced walls with round-headed windows, featuring cherub heads as keystones

Interior

- Simple rectangle with no aisles and blue-painted ceiling

- Finely carved original reredos, flanked by stone figures of Moses and Aaron, from All Hallows the Great (dem. 1894)

- Original pulpit, lectern and Royal Arms of William III on organ gallery

- Magnificent C17 brass chandelier from All Hallows the Great

- Striking modern stained glass windows by John Hayward, depicting the confrontation between good and evil, with St. Michael overcoming Satan in the central east window, flanked by windows depicting the Virgin and Child (shown spearing a dragon) and the angel Gabriel with Adam and Eve. The window in the south-west of the nave shows Dick Whittington and his cat, with the streets of London paved in gold

Summary

St Michael Paternoster Royal enjoys a picturesque setting behind the formal Whittington Garden which shelters the church somewhat from the busy Upper Thames Street. It was one of the last of Wren's City churches to be built and the last to be restored after the War.

The church will always be thought of in connection with Richard Whittington, who paid for its rebuilding and who worshipped and was buried here. Alas, the story of the cat is apocryphal, unless it refers to a "catte" or coastal boat owned by Whittington, who was a prosperous businessman.

The interior has some fine original woodcarving, but the blue ceiling and the stained glass windows, although beautiful in their own right, are not in keeping with Wren's original style and intentions. The exterior, however, provides a good example of the work of Wren's office, with original 17th century tower and walls, together with a most delicate and graceful steeple.

St Nicholas Cole Abbey

Queen Victoria Street

History

- Dedicated to the patron saint of children (also known as Santa Claus)

- "Cole Abbey" is probably a corruption of "Cold Harbour", a medieval shelter for travellers

- Rebuilt by Wren, 1672-78

- Gutted by bombing in WW2 and restored by Arthur Bailey, 1961-62

Exterior

- Built in Portland stone and situated prominently on Queen Victoria Street

- Round-headed windows under straight hoods on brackets

- Stone balustrade encircling the parapet

- North-west tower with trumpet-shaped steeple, iron balcony near the top and gilded weathervane in the shape of a ship, from St Michael Queenhythe (dem. 1876)

Interior

- An open rectangle with flat ceiling and plain walls embellished with gilt Corinthian pilasters

- Some C17 woodwork, including communion rails, pulpit and font cover by Richard Kedge

- South doorcase with carvings from the original reredos
- West gallery with C17 Royal Arms and three doorcases below, decorated with carvings, including cherub heads, also from the reredos
- Mid-C18 brass chandelier
- Wrought iron sword-rest, 1747
- Medieval carved stone head, discovered during restoration, behind panel by south doorcase
- Rich stained glass east windows by Keith New, 1962, depicting the extension of the Church overseas, with plaster swags above

Summary

St Nicholas Cole Abbey is a reminder of how so many City churches, formerly hidden behind house and offices in the narrow streets of the old City, have been exposed to public view in a way never envisaged by their builders.

Until Queen Victoria Street was developed in the 1860s, the main entrance to the church was from the north, in Distaff Lane (formerly Fish Street). The area was, for many centuries, the centre of the City's fish market. Today, the church is most easily seen from the south, where it stands above the street in a somewhat isolated position.

At one time, it acquired the nickname of "St Nicholas Cole Hole Abbey" because of the smoke created by the steam trains of the underground railway, which passed beneath.

A reminder of the severity of the Great Plague of 1665 is provided by the chilling statistic that over 90 of the 120 parishioners died from the disease in that year.

St Olave Hart Street
Hart Street

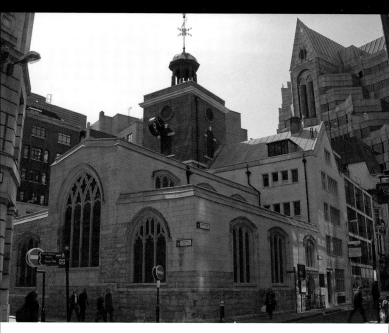

History

- Dedicated to Olave, King of Norway, who was killed fighting pagans. King Olave is remembered for assisting Ethelred the Unready against the Danish invaders by using his ships to pull down London Bridge in 1014, thus preventing the Danes from crossing the river and giving rise to the nursery rhyme, "London Bridge is falling down"

- Escaped the Great Fire, thanks mainly to the action of Samuel Pepys and William Penn Senior, who destroyed surrounding buildings to create a fire-break

- Severely damaged in WW2 and skilfully restored by Ernest Glanfield, 1951-54

Exterior

- C15 tower and aisles

- Churchyard in Seething Lane, with gates of 1658, featuring skulls, crossbones and spikes, causing Dickens, in The Uncommercial Traveller, to call the church "St Ghastly Grim"

Interior

- C15 walls and arcades, with a remarkable vestry in south-east corner dating from 1662, featuring C15 doorcase and a fine decorated plaster ceiling

- C13 crypt, housing an ancient well

- Small modern sculpture of St Olave in niche in south-west corner

- Modern reredos by Glanfield, with C17 communion rails

- Wren-period pulpit from St Benet Gracechurch Street (dem. 1867)

- Four sword-rests, two from All Hallows Staining (dem. 1870)

- Stained glass by A. E. Buss, 1953, with St Olave in left light of east window

- Window in north aisle depicting the Virgin Mary flanked by Queen Elizabeth I and St Katharine with (above) Elizabeth Fry, Florence Nightingale, Josephine Butler and Edith Cavell

- Fine monuments to James Deane (above vestry door), Andrew and Paul Bayninge (north side of sanctuary), Elizabeth Pepys (above north side of altar) and Samuel Pepys (south aisle, above site of former galleried Navy Office pews, entered from the churchyard)

Summary

St Olave is a rare survivor in the City of a typical medieval parish church and it has a wonderfully intimate feel from the moment that the visitor descends the short flight of steps from Hart Street into the nave.

Described by Samuel Pepys as *"our own church"*, it provided the final resting place for the great diarist and his wife. Their monuments are quite intriguing, with Elizabeth, above the sanctuary, staring directly down at Samuel in the south aisle, as if reprimanding him for his wayward behaviour.

There are several other fine monuments in the church, notably the Bayninge brothers, two colourful statues kneeling at prayer in a semicircular monument, looking like the automated figures on a great clock, ready to move round when the hour strikes.

St Olave combines plenty of original historic features with one of the most sensitive of the post-war restorations in the City.

St Peter Cornhill
St Peter's Alley, off Cornhill

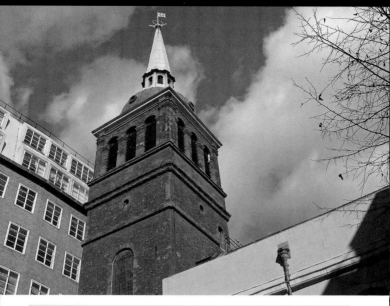

History

- Situated on what is generally considered to be the highest ground in the City and near the centre of the original Roman settlement

- Named Cornhill after the local corn market

- According to legend, the oldest Christian church in the City, supposedly founded by King Lucius in 179 AD

- Rebuilt by Wren, 1677-84

Exterior

- Hidden behind buildings in Cornhill, with a classical east façade on Gracechurch Street

- Stuccoed south wall facing churchyard in St. Peter's Alley

- Red brick tower with three round-headed openings on upper part of each side, capped by a small leaded dome supporting a lantern and obelisk copper-clad spire

- Original weather-vane in shape of St Peter's key

Interior

- Barrel-vaulted nave of five bays with two narrow aisles

- West gallery with Father Smith organ

- Four fine original doorcases at west end

- Magnificent wooden chancel screen (said by some to be jointly designed by Wren and his daughter)

- Reredos with unusual decorated pediment, featuring the Lamb of Sacrifice and the tetragrammaton (the Divine name in Hebrew characters) in a glory

- Large pulpit with richly carved tester

- Original C17 octagonal font and cover with a carved dove and cherub heads

- Monument (chancel, south wall) to seven children of James Woodmason who died in a fire while he was at a ball at St James Palace, the memorial featuring seven cherub heads and said to be designed by Francesco Bartolozzi

- Breadshelves in vestibule, used for distribution of bread to the poor

- Bright stained glass in east windows from Victorian restoration, with modern glass in aisles commemorating various army regiments associated with the church

Summary

Like its neighbour, St Michael Cornhill, St Peter is partially hidden behind nearby buildings, but a good view of the south side and the steeple can be seen from the little churchyard in St Peter's Alley. The east wall, on Gracechurch Street, is a rare example of Wren designing an elaborate east façade because of its visibility from a road or public thoroughfare (compare St Lawrence Jewry and St Mary at Hill).

St Peter's was the churchyard mentioned by Dickens in Our Mutual Friend, where *"the dead are raised above the living"*, a reference to the fact that the path is lower than the graveyard. In this spot, Lizzie Hexham resisted the unwelcome marriage proposal of Bradley Headstone.

The church itself has an attractive interior, with exceptional plasterwork and some very fine original furnishings. These include the carved wooden chancel screen, one of only two in the City, the other being in St Margaret Lothbury. Also worthy of special note are the fine pulpit and tester and magnificent west gallery.

St Sepulchre without Newgate

Holborn Viaduct

History

- Properly known as the Church of the Holy Sepulchre, after the Holy Sepulchre in Jerusalem

- First mentioned in 1137, rebuilt mid C15 by Sir John Popham, Chancellor of Normandy and Treasurer to King Henry VI

- Rebuilt again after the Great Fire, though not by Wren

- Heavy restoration in C19, but escaped serious damage in WW2

Exterior

- Massive Gothic tower, restored in early C18, with oversize pinnacles from late C19

- Aisles faced in Portland stone, with C17 sundial on south parapet and watch-house for deterring body-snatchers at east end

- C15 three–storey south porch by Popham, refaced in late C19

- The City's oldest drinking fountain set into south-east of churchyard wall

Interior

- Original C15 fan-vaulted porch interior, with carved bosses at rib intersections

- 150ft long nave with flat ceiling, separated from groin-vaulted north and south aisles by Tuscan arcades

- C17 reredos with segmental pediment

- Matching pulpit (right of nave) and reading desk (left)

x

- C17 churchwardens' pews (west end)

- C18 Royal Arms (south aisle)

- Renatus Harris organ with magnificent late C18 organ case

- Marble font of 1670 with ogee-shaped cover (south aisle); second finely carved font cover, decorated with cherub heads, from Christ Church in nearby Newgate Street (north end of vestibule)

- Fine C18 wrought iron communion rails and sword-rest

- Many excellent stained glass windows, including one to Dame Nellie Melba, by Brian Thomas (north chapel) and another to Captain John Smith, first Governor of Virginia, (south aisle), who is buried here

Summary

St Sepulchre, the largest of the City parish churches, stands prominently opposite the Old Bailey. It is a medieval church, largely rebuilt after the Great Fire, but heavily Victorianised. Some 15th century elements remain in the north and south walls and, notably, in the porch interior.

The notorious Newgate Gaol stood on the site now occupied by the Old Bailey and, at midnight before a day of executions, the sexton would pass through an underground passage from the church and ring his handbell (preserved in a glass case at the south-east of the nave), while reciting lines urging repentance and ending with the words *"And when St Sepulchre's bell in the morning tolls, The Lord have mercy on your souls"*.

The Musicians Chapel is evidence of the church's many musical connections, with Sir Henry Wood's ashes lying under the window to Saint Cecilia, patron saint of music. An adjacent window features Dame Nellie Melba, complete with peaches, recalling the dish to which she gave her name.

The church also has strong regimental connections and the evocative Loos Cross (north aisle) was brought from the First World War battlefield where 100 officers and men of the City of London Rifles perished in 1915.

History

- Built on the banks of the Walbrook river, (around which the Romans had founded Londinium in AD43), and first mentioned in the late C11

- Rebuilt by Wren, 1672-79

- Damaged by bombs in WW2 and restored by Godfrey Allen

- Restoration led by Lord Palumbo, 1978-87, following subsidence into the river Walbrook, with the introduction of a central altar and modern seating

Exterior

- Kentish ragstone tower, the upper part re-faced in Portland stone

- Three-stage steeple, recessed behind a balustrade, the lowest stage with three projecting columns on each corner. Similar to those at St James Garlickhythe and St Michael Paternoster Royal

- Copper-clad dome (the first to be built in this country, generally believed to be Wren's "trial run" for St Paul's)

- 12 steps up from the street, reflecting the church's position on the river bank

Interior

- A plain rectangle, but can also be seen as centrally-planned, like a Greek cross, with the dome rising above a square space, extended by an additional bay to form the nave

- 50-ton dome supported on eight semi-circular arches, in turn standing on four groups of three slender Corinthian columns, with four similar columns completing the nave

- Irregularly rounded altar by Henry Moore, made of Travertine and surrounded by modern beechwood seating by Andrew Varah

- Fine Wren-period woodwork, including reredos, communion table and rails, pulpit and tester carved by William Newman

- West doors carved by Jonathan Maine

- Font by Thomas Strong, with elaborate octagonal cover carved by Newman

- West gallery with organ case by G.P. England, 1765

Summary

A church which has been described as having the most perfectly-proportioned interior in the world, St Stephen Walbrook has the power to take one's breath away. Full of light, its design testifies to Wren's background as a mathematician, with rectangles, squares, circles, semi-circles and triangles creating a wonderful geometrical harmony. The dome and the groups of elegant classical columns are truly inspirational.

Although the central altar, a fine piece of work in its own right, is alien to the spirit of Wren's original design, it does not detract from the overall impact of an interior where one's instinct is to look up rather than down and where there is also some outstanding woodcarving to admire.

The church has several interesting associations. Sir John Vanbrugh, the great architect, is buried here, although he has no monument. The 16th century rector, Henry Pendleton, was immortalised as the "Vicar of Bray" and the Samaritans were founded in the church in 1953 by the rector, Chad Varah. The telephone used for the first call is displayed on a plinth in the south-west corner.

St Vedast alias Foster

Foster Lane, off Cheapside

History

- Dedicated to a C6 Flemish saint, Foster being an English corruption of the name

- Not completely destroyed by the Great Fire and restored without Wren's involvement, 1669-72

- Rebuilt by Wren, 1695-1701

- Gutted by bombing in WW2 and restored by Stephen Dykes-Bower, 1953-63

Exterior

- Remains of medieval walls at south-west corner and at east end

- Exceptional Portland stone steeple with first a concave, then a convex stage, each with clusters of pilasters at the corners and topped by an obelisk spire

- Secluded courtyard with wall-fountain and part of a Roman tessellated pavement displayed on the south wall, along with several other interesting items

Interior

- Rectangular nave, with clerestory, divided from south aisle by an arcade of Tuscan columns, screened off to form a separate chapel

- Black and white marble floor

- Richly decorated gold leaf and silver aluminium ceiling, with elaborate wreaths of leaves and flowers in gilded rectangles

- Reredos and communion rail from St Christopher le Stocks (dem. 1781)

- Collegiate-style seating

- Richly carved octagonal pulpit, with fruit and flowers, lions and skulls, from All Hallows Bread Street (dem. 1875)

- C18 organ-case from St Bartholomew by the Exchange (dem. 1841)

- Font and cover from St Anne and St Agnes

- Late C17 sword-rest, also from St Anne and St Agnes

- Stained glass east window by Brian Thomas, 1961

- Royal Arms from St Matthew Friday Street (dem. 1886)

- In south aisle, a late C17 communion table, also from St Matthew Friday Street, a remarkable aumbry by Bernard Merry, 1992 and a sculpture of Dove and Glory, with eight cherub heads, by Edward Strong, 1697

Summary

St Vedast is most notable for its fine steeple, often attributed to Nicholas Hawksmoor, although there is little direct evidence to support this. It is a distinct contrast to St Mary le Bow, which can be seen down Cheapside, and to Christ Church Newgate Street, visible in the opposite direction. The dome of St Paul's can also be seen close by.

St Vedast, though a post-war restoration inside, has many original 17th century furnishings, brought from other churches. In addition, it has some fine modern features, including an elaborately decorated ceiling.

Fountain Court, the delightful paved garden hidden away on the north side, entered from Foster Lane, is also not to be missed. Jacob Epstein's stone relief of the head of Canon Mortlock, a rector of the church, is among the items displayed on the walls of the courtyard. Also displayed is an Assyrian baked brick with very rare cuneiform inscription, found during excavations at the Zigurrat of Kalhu, carried out by the archaeologist Sir Max Mallowan, the second husband of Agatha Christie, who worshipped at St Vedast.

Temple Church
Middle and Inner Temple, off Fleet Street

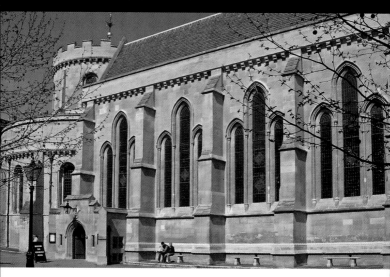

History

- Dedicated to St Mary the Virgin and named after the Knights Templar, a crusading order who settled in this area, c.1160

- Nave and porch built c.1160-85, chancel c.1220-40

- Taken over by the lawyers, who later settled in the area, as their private chapel

- Re-furnished by Wren, 1682

- Several restorations in C19 and, after bomb damage in WW2, by Walter H. Godfrey in 1947-57

Exterior

- Circular nave and rectangular chancel, set back from an open courtyard close to the buildings of the Inner and Middle Temple

- Walls re-faced in Bath stone in C19 restorations

- Rib-vaulted west porch and richly decorated, round-headed Norman doorway

Interior

- C12 circular nave in "Transitional " style (part Norman, part Gothic), featuring Purbeck marble piers supporting pointed arches, with round-headed arches in the triforium and clerestory

- Fine series of C13 effigies of knights in Purbeck marble, one original (Robert de Ros, 1227) the remainder restored

- Magnificent, classically-proportioned C13 chancel in Early English style, with aisles the same height as the nave

- Purbeck marble piers supporting a fine rib-vaulted chancel ceiling

- "Penitential cell" with two slit windows, in north-west corner of chancel

- Reredos carved by William Emmett, the only surviving part of Wren's re-furnishing

- Modern organ, 1954, replacing Father Smith instrument destroyed in WW2

- Intricate stained glass east windows by Carl Edwards, 1957-58

- Purbeck marble effigy of a bishop in south aisle, thought to be either Sylvester of Carlyle, d.1255, or Patriarch Heraclius

- Elaborately decorated alabaster altar-tomb to Edmund Plowden, 1584, Treasurer of Middle Temple (north side, between chancel and nave)

- Large, colourful monument to Richard Martin, 1615, Recorder of London, shown kneeling with an open book (south side, between chancel and nave)

Summary

Temple Church is a building of great architectural and historical significance. It is a fine example of the transition from the Norman to the Gothic style of architecture and is one of the earliest examples of Gothic in the country.

The rare circular Norman nave was built for the Knights' Templar in imitation of the Church of the Holy Sepulchre in Jerusalem and was consecrated by Patriarch Heraclius of Jerusalem in 1185. The beautiful 13th century chancel is widely praised for its perfect proportions and is a fine example of Early English architecture.

The church has achieved recent fame through Dan Brown's "Da Vinci Code", which has led many visitors to study the series of marble effigies of knights which lie on the floor of the nave. It is also well-known for its tradition of fine music, with regular recitals being given on its highly-acclaimed organ.

Christ Church Newgate Street

Newgate Street

History

- Built on the site of the chancel of the Franciscan (Greyfriars) monastery, after its dissolution in 1538

- Christ's Hospital ("Bluecoat") School established on remainder of site (relocated to Horsham, 1902)

- Church rebuilt by Wren, 1677-91

- Interior destroyed by bombing in WW2, the steeple restored by Lord Mottistone in 1960

- Nave turned into a garden by the City of London Corporation in 1989

- Tower converted to a private residence in 2006

Summary

Several medieval English queens were benefactors of the Greyfriars monastery and are buried on this site. These include Margaret, the second wife of Edward I and Isabella, wife of Edward II and complicit in his murder. Henry III's queen, Eleanor, asked for her heart to be buried here and Elizabeth Barton, the Holy Maid of Kent, was also buried on the site after being hanged at Tyburn for preaching against Henry VIII's marriage to Anne Boleyn.

The steeple is one of Wren's finest, *"a square version of St Mary le Bow"* says Pevsner. It consists of three square stages, the louvred belfry section giving rise to a central stage encircled by an open Ionic colonnade topped by 12 urns and, above them, a delicate square spire capped with a vase.

The old site of the monastery was taken over by the famous Christ's Hospital school, whose boys used the north gallery of the church when attending services. After the school moved out of London in 1902, the General Post Office buildings occupied the site. In recent years, these have given way to the offices of Merrill Lynch, the U.S. investment bank.

The church was not rebuilt after the War, but the nave has been made into a rose garden, using the footprint of the old church, the paths being on the lines of the former aisles, the pergolas where the piers used to be, the box hedging marking the pew area and the rose bushes the congregation.

St Dunstan in the East

St Dunstan's Hill off Lower Thames Street

History

- One of two City churches dedicated to the C10 Archbishop of Canterbury, the other being at the far end of Fleet Street

- One of the wealthiest medieval churches in the City, St Dunstan in the East survived the Great Fire, Wren only needing to rebuild the tower and steeple

- Body of the church rebuilt in early C19, but gutted by bombs in WW2

- Laid out as a garden by the City of London Corporation in 1967

Summary

Once one of the wealthiest and most prosperous churches in the City, St Dunstan in the East was not rebuilt after being gutted by bombs in the War.

The steeple, with its lantern and spire rising from the pinnacled tower on four flying buttresses, is one of Wren's most elegant creations, built in the Gothic style to match the body of the church, which survived the Great Fire. Wren's daughter is said to have had some influence on the design. When news that a storm in 1703 had caused damage to many City steeples, Wren apparently remarked *"not St Dunstan's, I am sure"*.

The ruins of the church were turned into a garden by the City of London Corporation in 1967. Today, this place of peace and quiet, where City workers can enjoy their lunch, is surely the most beautiful and evocative garden in the City. It features a small bubble fountain surrounded by a host of unusual trees, shrubs and flowers growing amongst the ruined arches, which are themselves covered in swathes of Virginia Creeper.

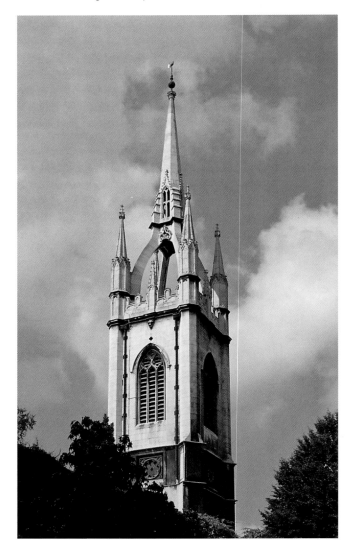

The church was formerly known as St Augustine with St Faith, the latter being a chapel in the crypt of St Paul's until the parishes were combined after the Great Fire. Before the development of New Change, Watling Street extended west as far as the cathedral.

Wren rebuilt the church and tower with the intention that the steeple, like St Martin Ludgate, should act as a counterpoint to the great dome of St Paul's. Although the church was destroyed by Second World War bombing, the tower survived and the steeple was restored, in fibreglass, in 1966.

The tower was incorporated into the Cathedral Choir School when the school was built on the adjacent site in 1962-67.

St Martin Orgar
Martin Lane, off Cannon Street

This red-brick, Italianate tower was built by John Davies in 1851-53 as a rectory for St Clement Eastcheap. It is not strictly speaking a church tower, but stands next to a small garden which was formerly the churchyard of St Martin Orgar. The original church was largely burnt down in the Great Fire, although its tower stood until the mid-19th century.

The present tower has a prominent clock, dated 1853, projecting on a bracket over the street.

St Mary Somerset
Upper Thames Street

Possibly named after a certain Ralph de Sumery, or a local wharf, Summer's Hythe, the church was one of Wren's last City churches, built in 1685-94. It was demolished in 1871, but the tower was considered to be of outstanding merit and allowed to survive. It is of four stages, with alternate circular and round-headed windows. On top of the tower are eight pinnacles, with panelled bases and little scrolls. The four corner pinnacles are topped with square fluted vases, while the four central ones are 20ft high obelisks, capped with balls.

A neatly planted garden has been created to the east of the tower, with horizontal rows of box and yew hedging, plus tall, slim maidenhair (ginkgo) trees echoing the elegant lines of Wren's tower.

There are discussions taking place about turning the tower into a residence, along the lines of Christ Church Newgate Street and St Alban Wood Street.

St Olave Jewry

Ironmonger Lane

Wren's church was demolished towards the end of the 19th century and the tower, with its battered (inwardly inclining) walls, Doric doorcase and tall obelisk corner pinnacles, is today used as offices. The churchyard remains as a beautiful garden, surrounded by iron railings.

Many of the furnishings from the church, including the exceptionally fine font, can be seen in St Margaret Lothbury, with which the parish was united.

St Margaret also has a bust of Alderman John Boydell, a Lord Mayor and the greatest print publisher of his day, who was buried at St Olave Jewry and who was known to walk down Ironmonger Lane every morning at 5am, hang his wig on top of the pump outside the church and sluice his head in cold water.

City Temple

Holborn Viaduct

This Congregational (URC) church was the second-largest non-conformist chapel in London when built in 1873-74 by Lockwood and Mawson, Yorkshire architects best known for their Bradford Town Hall.

Following severe bomb damage in the Second World War, the church was rebuilt to designs by Lord Mottistone of Seeley and Paget in 1955-58. A concrete framed building, with stone panels, was inserted between the original Bath stone end bays and tower, with its elaborate restored cupola.

The interior is a large hall, dominated by the pulpit and the great apse, around which are slim cedar columns, with a round window by Hugh Easton.

The Dutch Church

Austin Friars

The monastery church of the Austin (Augustine) Friars was founded on this site in 1253 and rebuilt after 1354. Following the dissolution of the monasteries, the surviving nave of the church was given to the Dutch Protestants who had arrived in London in large numbers during the 16th century. The church was restored in the 1860s and destroyed by bombing in the Second World War.

The church was rebuilt by Arthur Bailey, 1950-54, as a collection of rectangular boxes at different levels, all in Portland stone and surmounted by a lantern, small, slender spire and weathercock.

The interior is also on different levels, with a meeting hall below and the church itself on the first floor. It is simple and elegant, with a shallow, coffered vault, fluted pilaster strips on the walls and tall rectangular windows. A bright banner hangs from the pulpit above the communion table, beneath which can be seen fragments of the altar stone from the original church of 1253.

There is a fine, tall Tree of Life tapestry by Hans van Norden on the south wall and some excellent stained glass, particularly the west window by Max Nauta. Also worthy of note is the beautifully-crafted tubular-steel-framed spiral staircase to the organ, placed above the entrance doorway.

Possibly named after a certain Ralph de Sumery, or a local wharf, Summer's Hythe, the church was one of Wren's last City churches, built in 1685-94. It was demolished in 1871, but the tower was considered to be of outstanding merit and allowed to survive. It is of four stages, with alternate circular and round-headed windows. On top of the tower are eight pinnacles, with panelled bases and little scrolls. The four corner pinnacles are topped with square fluted vases, while the four central ones are 20ft high obelisks, capped with balls.

A neatly planted garden has been created to the east of the tower, with horizontal rows of box and yew hedging, plus tall, slim maidenhair (ginkgo) trees echoing the elegant lines of Wren's tower.

There are discussions taking place about turning the tower into a residence, along the lines of Christ Church Newgate Street and St Alban Wood Street.

St Olave Jewry

Ironmonger Lane

Wren's church was demolished towards the end of the 19th century and the tower, with its battered (inwardly inclining) walls, Doric doorcase and tall obelisk corner pinnacles, is today used as offices. The churchyard remains as a beautiful garden, surrounded by iron railings.

Many of the furnishings from the church, including the exceptionally fine font, can be seen in St Margaret Lothbury, with which the parish was united.

St Margaret also has a bust of Alderman John Boydell, a Lord Mayor and the greatest print publisher of his day, who was buried at St Olave Jewry and who was known to walk down Ironmonger Lane every morning at 5am, hang his wig on top of the pump outside the church and sluice his head in cold water.

City Temple

Holborn Viaduct

This Congregational (URC) church was the second-largest non-conformist chapel in London when built in 1873-74 by Lockwood and Mawson, Yorkshire architects best known for their Bradford Town Hall.

Following severe bomb damage in the Second World War, the church was rebuilt to designs by Lord Mottistone of Seeley and Paget in 1955-58. A concrete framed building, with stone panels, was inserted between the original Bath stone end bays and tower, with its elaborate restored cupola.

The interior is a large hall, dominated by the pulpit and the great apse, around which are slim cedar columns, with a round window by Hugh Easton.

The Dutch Church

Austin Friars

The monastery church of the Austin (Augustine) Friars was founded on this site in 1253 and rebuilt after 1354. Following the dissolution of the monasteries, the surviving nave of the church was given to the Dutch Protestants who had arrived in London in large numbers during the 16th century. The church was restored in the 1860s and destroyed by bombing in the Second World War.

The church was rebuilt by Arthur Bailey, 1950-54, as a collection of rectangular boxes at different levels, all in Portland stone and surmounted by a lantern, small, slender spire and weathercock.

The interior is also on different levels, with a meeting hall below and the church itself on the first floor. It is simple and elegant, with a shallow, coffered vault, fluted pilaster strips on the walls and tall rectangular windows. A bright banner hangs from the pulpit above the communion table, beneath which can be seen fragments of the altar stone from the original church of 1253.

There is a fine, tall Tree of Life tapestry by Hans van Norden on the south wall and some excellent stained glass, particularly the west window by Max Nauta. Also worthy of note is the beautifully-crafted tubular-steel-framed spiral staircase to the organ, placed above the entrance doorway.

Jewin Welsh Church

Fann Street

Named after an earlier chapel in Jewin Crescent, on the site of the Barbican, this Welsh Presbyterian church was built in 1956-61 by Caroe and Partners. It consists of a brick rectangular hall, south-west tower and copper-clad roof.

Inside the church, there is a central pulpit, above which is the organ. On the other three sides are traditional U-shaped galleries. The roof is supported by pointed concrete arches. The stained glass is by Carl Edwards.

St Etheldreda

Ely Place

St Etheldreda, just beyond the City's boundary near Holborn Circus, has been a Catholic church since 1874, when it was acquired by the Fathers of the Institute of Charity, (the Rosminians). It is a rare and outstanding example of medieval church building in the Decorated style. Dedicated to a 7th century Saxon Abbess who built a monastery at Ely, it was built as a private chapel in c.1293 for the Bishop of Ely, whose London home was on this site.

The undercroft of the church, which dates back to 1251, has stone piers with timber supports for the vault and, on the walls, modern carved reliefs of the Stations of the Cross.

The church above has Gothic arcading along the walls of the nave, with modern painted statues of Catholic martyrs. The modern stained glass throughout the church is considered to be some of the best in the country, particularly in the great east and west windows,

which retain their elaborate late 13th century tracery and which are among the largest stained glass windows in London.

St George's German Lutheran Church
Alie Street

Situated just outside the City, St George's is the oldest surviving German church in the country. It was founded in 1763 by Dederich Beckmann, a wealthy sugar-baker, who established the church to provide for the spiritual needs of the many German Protestant refugees in London, as well as the large numbers of young men who came from the north German Hanseatic towns to work in the rapidly-growing Whitechapel sugar-refining industry.

Although it survived the Second World War, the church fell into disrepair after its congregation moved away to unite with St Mary's Lutheran Church in Bloomsbury, but it was restored by the Historic Chapels Trust and re-opened in 2004.

St George's is hardly altered from the time when it was built and features box-pews of the type once common in the City churches. The pulpit, commandment boards and gilt arms of King George III are all original, as is the rare painted canvas reredos. The beautiful Crucifixion window in the south (ritual west) wall has borders of stamped jewel glass, the first-known example of this technique, and was made by Powell and Sons in 1855.

St Mary Moorfields

Eldon Street

The only purpose-built Roman Catholic church in the City, (by George Sherrin, 1899-1903), St Mary Moorfields does not, at first sight, look like a church. Its Portland stone south front (the church is aligned on a north-south axis) is set between commercial buildings in Eldon Street, but an elaborate carving of the Virgin and Child above the arched portal indicates what lies inside.

The barrel-vaulted interior, of four bays, has an apse in the north (ritual east) end. The marble altar comes from the church's predecessor, built in 1817-20. On either side of the altar are pairs of Corinthian columns from an 1852 refitting of the earlier building. Above the entrance to the north-west chapel, dedicated to Sir Thomas More, is a mosaic lunette depicting More's execution.

Spanish and Portuguese Synagogue

Off Bevis Marks

This is the oldest surviving English synagogue, built in 1699-1701 by a Quaker, Joseph Avis. It replaced the synagogue in nearby Creechurch Lane, which was the first place of worship used by the Jews when Oliver Cromwell's Commonwealth allowed them to re-settle in England, almost four centuries after their expulsion by Edward I in 1290.

The synagogue is set in a small courtyard off Bevis Marks. It has a plain, red brick exterior, which gives little indication of the exceptional beauty inside. Round-headed, plain glass windows throw light into the rectangular interior, where there are lattice-fronted galleries on three sides, supported on Tuscan columns, and seven magnificent, low-hanging brass chandeliers.

At the east end is a two-storeyed Echal, similar to a Wren-period reredos, in the upper part of which are the painted letters of the Decalogue, in Hebrew. The Echal incorporates the Ark, which houses the Torah scrolls and is surrounded by rails, on which are five of the brass candlesticks representing the Ten Commandments. The other five are on the rails around the reading platform, the Bimah, towards the west end of the synagogue.

An extension was built to the south of the synagogue by Thomas Ford in 2001, which incorporates an open-roofed Sukkah and a kosher restaurant.

Aedicule: a frame around a doorway, niche or window, with two columns supporting a pediment

Apse: a semicircular vaulted space, normally at eastern end of a church

Arcade: series of arches on piers or columns. Arcading: the same applied to a wall surface

Attic storey: a storey above the main entablature on a classical facade

Aumbry: recess or cupboard for containing the vessels used for Holy Communion

Baldacchino: free-standing canopy over an altar

Barrel-vault: see Vaults

Chantry: a chapel where prayers were said for the soul of a founder or benefactor

Corbel: a stone bracket or support

Clerestory: uppermost storey of the nave containing a row of windows

Coffering: sunken panels decorating a ceiling or arch

Composite: see Orders

Corinthian: see Orders

Decorated: the style of Gothic architecture from late C13 to mid C14

Doric: see Orders

Early English: the style of Gothic architecture in the C12 and C13

Entablature: see Orders

Festoon: ornamental garland

Gadroon: ribbed ornamentation, like inverted fluting

Groin-vault: see Vaults

Header: brick laid at right-angles to a wall

Ionic: see Orders

Ogee: double curve, bending first one way, then the other (i.e. partly convex, partly concave)

Oriel: window projecting from the upper storey of a wall, often supported by a bracket

Orders: the five styles of classical architecture, consisting of vertical columns surmounted by a horizontal section, the entablature. The three Greek orders were: Doric (simple stocky column with plain capital); Ionic (slender column with spiral scrolls on the capital); and

Corinthian (slender column with capital carved with acanthus leaves). The two Roman orders were Tuscan (slightly simpler version of Doric); and Composite (combining features of the Ionic and the Corinthian).

Pediment: triangular or segmental gable above a classical order, often above a portico or windows (a broken pediment having the upper central part omitted; an open pediment having the lower central part omitted)

Perpendicular: the style of Gothic architecture from mid C14 to early C16

Pilaster: shallow square classical column attached to a wall

Piscina: basin for washing communion vessels, usually to south of an altar

Quoins: dressed stones at the angle of a building

Reredos (or altar-piece): ornamental screen behind an altar

Rib-vault: see Vault

Rood: cross or crucifix, often on a rood-screen, separating nave from chancel

Rustication: deeply channelled masonry, to give an impression of strength

Sedilia: recessed stone seats for priests on the south side of the chancel

Sword-rests: elaborate wrought iron (or, occasionally, wooden) poles or frames, normally on the front pews, for the sword of office of the Lord Mayor on official visits

Tessellated: made of small pieces of mosaic

Tester (or sounding board): canopy over a pulpit

Tondo: circular carved or painted sculpture

Tracery: openwork pattern of masonry in the upper part of a window

Triforium: arcaded storey above nave or chancel and below clerestory

Trompe l'oeil: painted or architectural effect to give 3D impression on a flat surface and thus "deceive the eye"

Tympanum: space in the head of a doorway arch or pediment

Vault: arched stone roof, including: barrel-vault, a rounded vault, shaped like a tunnel; groin-vault, the junction of two barrel-vaults, intersecting at right angles; rib-vault, a framework of intersecting arches